MISSING
NEW ORLEANS

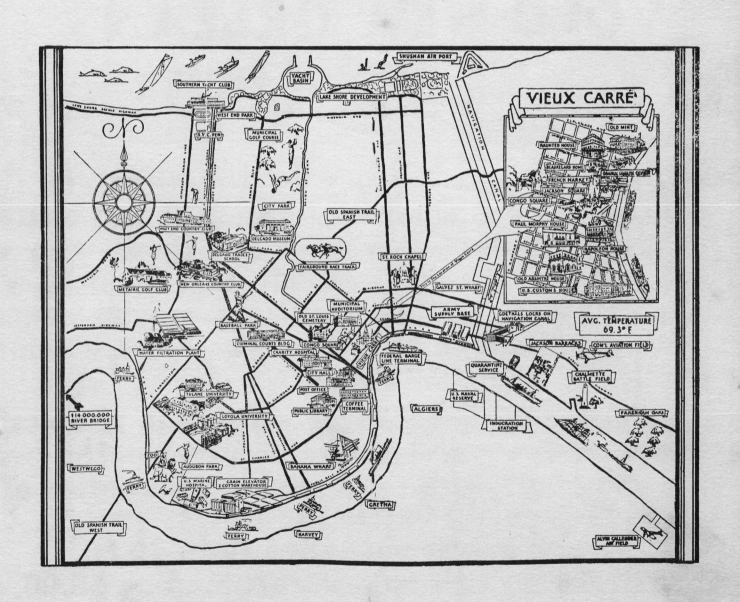

PHILLIP COLLIER'S
MISSING
NEW ORLEANS

FOREWORD BY
PETE FOUNTAIN

INTRODUCTIONS BY
J. RICHARD GRUBER

TEXT BY
JIM RAPIER & MARY BETH ROMIG

THE OGDEN MUSEUM OF SOUTHERN ART
university of new orleans

with support from

THE COLLECTION
The Historic New Orleans Collection

PUBLICATION OF THIS BOOK WAS MADE POSSIBLE WITH THE SUPPORT OF THE GOLDRING FAMILY FOUNDATION

SECOND PRINTING PUBLISHED WITH THE SUPPORT OF THE HISTORIC NEW ORLEANS COLLECTION

This book is published under the auspices of The Goldring-Woldenberg Institute for the Advancement of Southern Art and Culture, The Ogden Museum of Southern Art, University of New Orleans

www.ogdenmuseum.org

DESIGNED BY
Phillip Collier Designs, Phillip Collier, Dean Cavalier

COVER CONCEPT:
Phillip Collier, Will Crocker

COVER DESIGN:
Phillip Collier, Dean Cavalier

COVER IMAGE:
Photograph of the second St. Charles Hotel by George Francois Mugnier,
Glass plate negative from the collection of Mitchell Gaudet

First edition printed in the Metropolitan New Orleans area by Brennan's Printing
Pre-press by Yvette Schellhaas Tassin, Brennan's Printing
Second printing by Wetmore & Company, an RR Donnelley Company
Manufactured in the United States of America

09   08   07   06   05   04   03   02   01   00   4   3   2

Library of Congress Cataloging-in-Publication Data

Collier, Phillip, J. Richard Gruber, Jim Rapier, Mary Beth Romig
Missing New Orleans
Includes bibliographical references and index

ISBN 0-9772544-0-2

Library of Congress Control Number: 2005932255

SAN: 257-1161

▸ The master plan for Audubon Park was developed by John Charles Olmsted, of the well-known Massachusetts park-design firm founded by Frederick Law Olmsted. First observing the site in 1897, Olmsted was particularly impressed with the great oaks, noting that is was "difficult to exaggerate the value of such noble trees." But the designer created much controversy in 1916-1918, when his landscaping plans included the removal of "Lover's Lane," a straight row of trees that had grown quite popular.

Lovers Lane - Audubon Park.

HOTEL NEW ORLEANS
DRINK
REGAL
BEER
CLOTHES
LOEWS
ALWAYS ASK FOR
MOTHER'S
HOME MADE PIES
BREAD
Schiro's
SOLE AGENT FOR
CAPEZIO
DANCE FOOTWEAR
AMERICAN DRUGS
Sterling
ICE CREAM
LOEW'S
MGM'S "YEARLING"
GREGORY PECK
JANE WYMAN
CLAUDE JARMAN JR.
ROBBINS
HUDSON
6 ST. BERNARD
1446

TABLE OF CONTENTS

Automobile and streetcar traffic merge on Canal Street, the city's busiest thoroughfare in the late 1940s.

Canal Street at night (c. 1940s)

Café Des Exilés

A haven on Royal Street for those fleeing the French Revolution in 1789 and Haiti's 1794 slave rebellion, Café Des Exiles, an eatery housed in a one-and-a-half story Creole cottage, enjoyed its heyday in the mid-1830s. By the 1840s, exiles had become New Orleanians, and their wars had become memories, as had Café Des Exiles. Its story, however, was recorded in the 1880s in *Creole Days*, written by George W. Cable.

PROLOGUE

Over five years ago, the original idea for what was to become the book *Missing New Orleans* was conceived by Phillip Collier. Late in the spring of 2005, Collier, a collaborator with The Ogden Museum of Southern Art on graphic and design issues, brought his evolving concept for the book to the Museum. For many reasons, the Ogden Museum offered to publish the book with Collier. A tight deadline was set, and the publication's team, drawing upon the city's distinctive archival and research institutions, including The Historic New Orleans Collection, advanced the research, writing, editing and design work required to complete the book.

Its final proof form was scheduled to be delivered to Brennan's Printing in New Orleans on Wednesday, August 31, 2005. On Saturday, August 27, with news that a Category 5 hurricane was predicted to make landfall along the Louisiana coastline, the staff of the Ogden Museum executed the Museum's hurricane preparedness plan. And, like many other residents of the metropolitan New Orleans area, we evacuated the city, taking the final galleys of the book for safe-keeping and one last review. Hurricane Katrina hit the Louisiana and Mississippi coast early on Monday, August 29. Within 24 hours, the original meaning behind the title "Missing New Orleans" changed dramatically.

The Historic New Orleans Collection, dedicated to preserving Louisiana's cultural legacy for present and future generations, was the first cultural institution in the city to open its doors to the public following the hurricane. Soon thereafter, on October 27, the Ogden Museum reopened, joining The Historic New Orleans Collection in offering New Orleans residents and visitors an opportunity to experience the city and the South's unique culture – including the region's visual arts, music and history.

Undaunted by the many challenges that arose in the aftermath of the storm, the team behind the production of *Missing New Orleans*, along with the staff of Brennan's Printing, rededicated themselves to make the publication a reality. The original goal had been to unveil the book in early November. The book was released on November 19, 2005, at the Museum, accompanied by an exhibition of the same title. The first printing sold out in less than four weeks.

Missing New Orleans was honored by the Louisiana Endowment for the Humanities as a "Humanities Book of the Year" for 2005.

We are grateful for our ongoing partnership with The Historic New Orleans Collection. In addition to generously sharing their expertise and archival materials for the book's content, THNOC's Board of Directors and staff have joined the Ogden Museum as our publication partner in this second printing. This collaboration makes it possible for larger audiences to relive the rich history of the city once known as the "Queen of the South."

J. Richard Gruber, January 31, 2006

FOREWORD

PETE FOUNTAIN

New Orleans is my home, always has been, always will be. I was born in New Orleans, and besides a few years in California when I was on the Lawrence Welk Show, I've lived here most of my life. I even ran a music club on Bourbon Street for many years. Oh, the stories I could tell.

When I was growing up during the Depression and WWII era, the old ways still lingered. They were hard times for the nation, but there was so much going on here when I was a kid. Movies were a big thing. I used to listen to all the jazz bands going to the movie houses downtown. I would go to the Top Hat Dance Hall to hear Sharkey Romano, Louis and Leon Prima, and a lot of great bands playing there. I used to listen from outside the club as a kid. During my life, I have seen a lot of change in New Orleans, some for the better and some for the worse. Many of the old music clubs, musicians and neighborhood clubs are gone now. After the war, downtown flourished for a time, then that changed, and I watched landmarks disappear. People left the city, moved to the suburbs, shopped in malls, not on Canal Street. Yet, Bourbon Street was always alive for me. Bourbon Street is my love. I went through McDonogh 28 and Warren Easton schools. Then I went through the conservatory of Bourbon Street. Yes, Bourbon Street was my conservatory. I spent over 30 years there, and that's a long time off and on Bourbon Street.

When people ask me about the Quarter, I tell them it's like a roller coaster. It had its ups and downs. Some years it's really down, and then they clean it up and it goes up again. New Orleans is one of the world's most unique cities. I've been proud to represent her around the world. The city, like the Quarter, always seems to come back. After playing the music of New Orleans elsewhere, it always felt great to return home. In a way, Phillip Collier's *Missing New Orleans* is like a trip home for me, a visit back to what I remember from earlier times here. It reminds me not just of what is "missing," but of what still makes my city, New Orleans, one of the greatest places on earth. On the streets of New Orleans history still lives, and music remains in the air. I do my part to keep it there, especially every year during Mardi Gras, marching with my Half-Fast Walking club through the city's streets, playing to the crowds, passing the buildings, clubs and places I will always remember.

▼ In the spring of 1959, after spending time in California, Pete Fountain set up shop at the Bateau Lounge on Bourbon Street, where he fronted his own combo, and where he recorded the album *PETE FOUNTAIN At The BATEAU LOUNGE.* On the album's cover Fountain wrote, "... by and large the lure of this fascinating city has its effect on its native sons, and back they come to the sights, smell, sounds that combine in a distinctive aura that means home ... New Orleans."

◄ "Going to the movies" was a popular pastime during the years when Pete Fountain was growing up in New Orleans. The Globe Theater was among the movie palaces on Canal Street. By 1940, there were nearly 50 neighborhood movie houses throughout the city.

▲ A young Phillip Collier poses in front of the entrance to Pontchartrain Beach's Cockeyed Circus while vacationing with his family in New Orleans (circa 1957).

▲ A postcard from the Old Absinthe House commemorates the structure where the fictional detectives from the television series *Bourbon Street Beat* were supposed to have had offices.

PREFACE

Missing New Orleans, a project that traces its origins back to 1975 when I moved here from Birmingham, Alabama, reflects my vision and understanding of institutions and entities that have contributed to the history of this great city. Though no longer in existence, in some way they made their mark on the city or in the memories of those who experienced them. This is not intended to be a definitive text on this city's past; there are many excellent city histories published. Nor do I pretend to be a scholar in the field of New Orleans history. It is not comprehensive – if any book on New Orleans could ever be – as there are many other people, places and traditions that are not included in this book. However, I hope the reader will see through my eyes and experiences what a city of great images New Orleans is and has been.

Long before I moved to New Orleans, I believe I was destined to live here. I grew up in Montgomery, Alabama, and recall a family vacation to New Orleans in 1957, when I was seven years old, during which we visited the zoo, the French Quarter and Pontchartrain Beach. Back home, I would lie in bed at night listening to WWL, the city's powerful AM radio station, as they broadcast live music from the Roosevelt Hotel's Blue Room. I imagined what it looked like, until years later when I would find among my grandmother's possessions an old linen postcard from the Blue Room. It was mailed to her home in Lower Peachtree, Alabama during World War II from my Uncle C. E. Garrick, a waiter at the Blue Room and his wife, Vera, a waitress at Delmonico's on St. Charles Avenue.

During the late 1950s, I was obsessed with rock 'n roll music and would play my 45's of Shirlee and Lee's recording of *Let the Good Times Roll* and Fats Domino's *I'm Gonna Be a Wheel Someday* until the vinyl practically wore out. As a teenager, one of my favorite songs was *The House of the Rising Sun*, about a New Orleans bordello that was the "ruin of many a poor boy." I marveled at the fact that New Orleans was mentioned in so many songs, unaware that I was developing a love for the "New Orleans sound."

At the same time I was intrigued by two television shows – *Yancy Derringer*, about a riverboat gambler in post-Civil War New Orleans, and *Bourbon Street Beat*, set in New Orleans and featuring three dashing detectives with offices on the 2nd floor of the original Old Absinthe House. In 1969, I saw the movie *Easy Rider*, with its images of New Orleans cemeteries and the French Quarter, and found myself, while on a college road trip to the West Coast, having to pass through the city, searching for locations in the movie. But, my defining moment came in 1975, during a visit to New Orleans for the Jazz Fest. Attending an evening concert on the steamboat Admiral, I stood only three feet away from Fats Domino, looking up at him as he pounded on a grand piano, and my fate was clear. ... It's a story that I share with many others – I had to live in this great city. I quit my job and moved to New Orleans.

My first job was in a graphic design studio in the Old Jax Brewery stables on Wilkinson Row

in the French Quarter. In my new job, I found myself in the workplace listening to native New Orleanians – Robert Alford, Hugh Ricks, Jim Pertuit and Raul Esquivel among them – reminiscing with fondness about places that were landmarks for generations, places they knew from growing up in New Orleans, places that intrigued me but I could not experience because they were "missing." I grew increasingly curious, and often found myself during lunch walking around the French Quarter, looking for the site of the old French Opera House, the La Casas Marina Bar and the Morning Call Coffee Stand. I would drive to the lakefront and try to picture the New Basin Canal and Spanish Fort Amusement Park.

As I walked the French Quarter streets, I wondered how, in a city so steeped in history and rich with architecture, there could be so much missing. I am a graphic designer by trade, a visual thinker and a visual person. I wanted to "see" these places, to know where they were, what they looked like, and who the people were who inhabited them. I wanted to know what I had missed.

So, I listened to stories and, instilled with my mother's habit of collecting things and my father's passion for history, began acquiring images of these places long gone, vintage postcards, old photographs and drawings. I created research files on things as long gone as the original St. Louis and St. Charles Hotels, and as recently closed as Pontchartrain Beach. As my professional career in New Orleans evolved, I was fortunate to work for historic firms and institutions such as The Historic New Orleans Collection, Bauerlein Advertising, Tulane University, the New Orleans Museum of Art, and my files kept growing.

Eventually I opened my own design studio in Factor's Row, one floor above where Degas created his famous painting, *The Cotton Exchange in New Orleans* (1873). I shopped at D. H. Holmes, Maison Blanche and Godchaux's, and "made groceries" at Schwegmann's, spent many nights listening to music at the Absinthe Bar on Bourbon Street and the original Rosy's on Tchoupitoulas Street. I spent some memorable evenings at Lu and Charlie's Jazz Club on Rampart Street, one night talking with piano legend James Booker between sets. I've enjoyed eating at Fitzgerald's at West End and the old Delmonico's, and attended the Jazz Fest before it got too crowded. I spent nearly every night at the 1984 Louisiana World's Fair. I experienced the oil boom and its subsequent bust. I've dined with the now-deceased local historian John Chase at the Napoleon House and spent an afternoon with Willie Maylie, also deceased, at his former restaurant, talking about the old days of the Poydras Market.

Over the years, the stories and memories continued to unfold about this restaurant, that hotel, this product, that sporting event. At the same time, it began to feel as if each week I was reading in the local *Times-Picayune* newspaper about another New Orleans institution that was closing or dissolving its

▲ A postcard mailed to Phillip Collier's grandmother in Alabama, sent by his Uncle C. E. Garrick and wife, Vera, pictured above, celebrates the Blue Room's elegant atmosphere.

▲ Phillip Collier's destiny was forever altered during a Jazz Fest evening concert on the S. S. Admiral excursion steamer, featuring Fats Domino.

business. With this research collection ever-expanding, especially over the past five years, I began to see the possibilities for a book project, and realized this could be a way to pay tribute to what has passed – for good and bad.

Over the years I've worked with such institutions as Whitney and Hibernia banks, the Delta Queen Steamboat Company, the Audubon Zoo and Aquarium of the Americas, the New Orleans Tourism and Marketing Corporation and Brennan's Restaurant, and local hotels including the Windsor Court, the Bienville House, Le Pavillon and the historic Monteleone Hotel. In collaborating with The National D-Day Museum, Louisiana Children's Museum, the Contemporary Arts Center, the House of Blues, Pete Fountain, the Neville Brothers and others, I've been involved in developing logos and advertising that have helped to brand their names worldwide. And, I have been privileged to work with The Ogden Museum of Southern Art, the institution that has been instrumental in publishing this book, long before this national museum on the South opened to the public. Throughout my career, I have been fortunate to partner with many of these and other great people and organizations that continue to make this city so special. I have come to love this city and can't imagine living anywhere else.

In part, this book has been influenced by earlier illustrated histories of New Orleans, such as Leonard V. Huber's *New Orleans: A Pictorial History*, Mary Cabel's *Lost New Orleans* and Mel Leavitt's *A Short History of New Orleans*. Though many of these books are filled with fantastic images, they are far removed from the level of design and reproduction that modern audiences expect today. Seeing this, and realizing how much I have come to love this subject, I have attempted to create a volume visually worthy of the images and accompanying text, bringing them to local audiences and those interested in knowing more about New Orleans.

In reading this book, I hope readers will come to share my love for New Orleans. I met my wife, Cindie, here. She is also one of those transplants to the city after only one trip, originally from Arizona. Together we have established our home in New Orleans where we are raising our children, Riki and James. I have dragged my family, willingly and often unwillingly, to see the sites where many of these places presented in this book once stood, and have shared trivial facts with them about New Orleans. I am grateful to them for their patience in enduring my many mini-history lessons, and in appreciating them, or pretending to, as much as I do.

I also want to take the opportunity to remark on all that continues to make New Orleans a special place to call home – the continuing revitalization of the Warehouse Arts District, the potential revitalization of Lincoln Beach, the conversion of the old Customs House to the Audubon Nature Institute's Insectarium and the Ogden Museum's restoration of the historic Howard Memorial Library, now the Patrick F. Taylor Library, on Lee Circle – to name a few.

Phillip Collier, August 14, 2005

▲ A poster for Rosy's, by artist Milton Glaser, is indicative of the unique atmosphere the club promised its patrons.

ACKNOWLEDGEMENTS

First, I would like to thank Rick Gruber, Director of The Ogden Museum of Southern Art, University of New Orleans, who shared my vision for *Missing New Orleans* and made it possible to publish this book. In addition, his contributions to the text provided valuable information for placing much of this book's subject matter in historical context. Thanks as well to writers Mary Beth Romig and Jim Rapier, who worked under incredible deadlines to complete the text, adding the stories behind the images; and, to Mary Beth for her efforts in coordinating marketing, details and timelines, keeping the team on schedule.

From The Ogden Museum of Southern Art: Beverly Sakauye, Jan Katz, Liz Williams, Katherine Doss and Rose Macaluso for their assistance. To Joe Bergeron, for his contribution in sharing his photographs by Charles Weber from the Bergeron Gallery, and who took many photographs of objects for the book; and to photographers Frank Gordon, Bob Cole for lending their collections and work, and Mike Terranova for his photographs of objects included in the book. To collectors of New Orleans memorabilia: Henry Shane, Al Kleindienst, Bob Murret, Robert Laurent, Andrew P. Wood, Joey Stephens, Deville Book Store, Cohen Antiques, Mona Mia Antiques, Bruce Henderson, the Fairmont New Orleans Hotel for sharing their possessions. For their assistance in research: John Lawrence, John Magill and Sally Stassi, Historic New Orleans Collection; Dr. Florence Jumonville, University of New Orleans Earl K. Long Library Special Collections; Irene Wainwright and Wayne Everard, the New Orleans Public Library; and Tom Lanham, the Louisiana State Museum. For their guidance: Chancellor Tim Ryan, Dr. Raphael Cassimere and Sharon Gruber, University of New Orleans, Errol Laborde, Peggy Scott Laborde, John Kemp, Jerry Romig, Sydney Besthoff and John Lawrence. And, to Allen Marks, Marks Paper Company, and Matt Palmer, A to Z Paper, for their assistance in securing paper for this publication.

To my personal researchers, Cindie, Riki and James Collier, and Glen Collier, Brenda Collier and Maude Garrick for their assistance and support over the years. A special note of thanks to the late Danny Brennan, for his early commitment to this publication, and most recently to his son, Danny, and the team at Brennan's Printing—and to the late Hugh Ricks, my dear friend and a great New Orleans storyteller. To my colleague from Phillip Collier Designs, Scott Carroll, for his valuable book design advice. And to Dean Cavalier, of Phillip Collier Designs, who took my design ideas and improved upon them to give this book its distinctive look.

Finally, thank you to Bill Goldring, from the Goldring Family Foundation, for his belief in and support of *Missing New Orleans*.

ST LOUIS HOTEL IN 1904
CORNER of CHARTRES ST.

INTRODUCTION

New Orleans is a city recognized for its architectural and cultural heritage, as well as for an associated patina of age and decay. As one recent national travel guide suggests, this patina is a central part of the city's appeal: "One of the deepest pleasures of New Orleans is that it isn't new; it's old. Really old. It seems like it was old when it was built." [1] In his new book, *Feet on the Street, Rambles Around New Orleans*, Roy Blount also refers to the history of a city he has known for decades: "New Orleans is not what it once was, neither the fetid swamp nor the great city nor the readily affordable bohemia....But New Orleans is still itself enough to erase any doubt that it was all of the things it has been; it hasn't lost the feel. It's like no other place in America, and yet (or therefore) it's the cradle of American culture." [2]

New Orleans, as Blount indicates, is "like no other place in America." Attracting more than ten million visitors in 2004, many people travel to the city for its traditions and because it appears to have changed less than most American cities. However, as evident in Phillip Collier's new visual history, the city *has* changed, has remained in a process of continual evolution. Collier, a noted New Orleans designer, contemplated initiating this book project as he witnessed the city's evolution and as he heard countless stories about "missing" New Orleans over the years. As his history files and photographic archives for the project expanded, and as the stories continued to unfold, his concepts for a book took shape, with the current volume taking form over the past five years.

Since its founding, almost three hundred years ago, New Orleans has attracted a broad and diverse range of visitors and new residents, including notable writers, artists and photographers. As a result, while much of the city's architectural history and material culture has been lost, much has been preserved, and much has been recorded—in literature, in oral traditions and in the visual arts, including photographs and films. Looking through this book, one develops a greater understanding of the individuals who have populated the city, as well as an appreciation of its many "missing" historic structures, institutions and business enterprises.

In the 21st century, we are fortunate to be able to read the words of those who lived in or passed through the city during an earlier era, describing its neighborhoods and public structures, as well as its homes, clubs, restaurants and social organizations. During the 1850s, when New Orleans was known as the "Queen of the South," it was one of the nation's largest cities with America's second busiest port. In this period, Thomas Wharton, a supervising architect on the Customs House, then under construction on Canal Street, served as an acute observer who documented the city's life in his drawings and journals. He witnessed and described the construction of the new Robb mansion on Washington Avenue (demolished in 1954), an imposing Garden District home for one of the city's greatest entrepreneurs with a nationally significant art collection:

▼ In 1844, James Robb, a prominent resident of New Orleans, commissioned Thomas Sully to paint this *Portrait of Mrs. Robb and Her Three Children*, before his wife and one of his daughters succumbed to death and Robb fell on hard times. *(Ogden Museum Permanent Collection)*

◀ The painting *St. Louis Hotel*, by William Woodward, depicts the hotel on the left. The Girod House, in the center, was designed by the architect and painter Hyacinthe Laclotte and built in 1814 by Mayor Nicholas Girod, with the intention that it should become the home of Napoleon Bonaparte, after his rescue from St. Helen's Island where he was held prisoner by the British. While the St. Louis Hotel was demolished in 1915, the Girod House, now the Napoleon house, still stands. The building on the far right was known as Maspero's Exchange.
(Ogden Museum Permanent Collection)

A photograph of Louis Armstrong shows one of New Orleans' most famous citizens holding his instrument of choice, the trumpet. Among Armstrong's well-known songs was his rendition of *Do You Know What It Means to Miss New Orleans?*

A photograph of St. Charles Avenue, taken from the corner of Canal Street in 1910, includes the third St. Charles Hotel in the background. A small sign marks the entrance to Kolb's restaurant, which was eventually replaced by a larger sign that still exists, long after the restaurant ceased operation.
(Ogden Museum Permanent Collection)

Long walks in the afternoon amid the beautiful residences of the Fourth District. The air loaded with perfume, and comparatively free from the dust of the City. Mr. Robb's grand square mansion rapidly approaching completion, and the grounds around, comprising the entire square, already laid out in sweeping walks, and grass plots, parterres and groups of planting and embellished at suitable points with statues, and rich vases. A wide parapet, carefully sodded and faced with a high breast wall of solid masonry surrounds the house, and gives it an imposing effect. [3]

After the Civil War, New Orleans entered a very different period in its history. One of the authors often associated with the city during these years was Mark Twain, who, in *Life on the Mississippi* (1883), recorded his impressions not only of well-known areas, like the Mississippi River and the French Quarter, but also areas like Lake Pontchartrain, making reference to some of the lost structures featured in this book:

And by and by we reached the West End, a collection of hotels of the usual light summer-resort pattern, with broad verandas all around, and the waves of the wide and blue Lake Pontchartrain lapping the thresholds....Thousands of people come by rail and carriage to the West End and to Spanish Fort every evening, and dine, listen to the bands, take strolls in the open air under the electric lights, go sailing on the lake, and entertain themselves in various and sundry other ways. [4]

During the early 20th century, the city influenced many of that century's most significant figures. One of them was Louis Armstrong, who was raised in New Orleans and remembered the thriving district known as Storyville, which served as home to many noted jazz musicians and the prostitutes immortalized by Bellocq in his photographic survey of the area: "There were all kinds of thrills for me in Storyville. On every corner I could hear music. And such good music! The music I wanted to hear. It was worth my salary—the little I did get—just to go into Storyville. It seemed as though all the bands were shooting at each other with those hot rifts." [5] Storyville was closed by the Navy in 1917, and was eventually destroyed to make way for a public housing project.

During the years between World War I and World War II, many artists, writers and performing artists moved to New Orleans and the French Quarter, attracted by its cheap rents and Bohemian atmosphere. Many also recognized the changing character of the city, as indicated by Sherwood Anderson in 1922: "There is an old city here, on the lip of America, and all about it has been built a new and more modern city. In the old city a people once lived who loved to play, who made love in the moonlight, who walked under trees, gambled with death in the dueling fields. These people are pretty much gone now, but their old city is

still left. Men here call it the 'Vieux Carre.'" [6]

Lyle Saxon, a writer who was closely associated with the French Quarter and its art circles, published a classic book on the city, *Fabulous New Orleans*, in 1928. In a chapter titled "An Afternoon Walk," he offered his readers a guided tour of the French Quarter with specific reference to one of its recently destroyed landmarks, the St. Louis Hotel:

> *Come, let's be going. We must continue down Royal Street. Just beyond the court house at the corner of Royal and St. Louis streets on this empty stretch of ground there once stood the old St. Louis Hotel, sometimes called the Hotel Royal. In its day it was the most fashionable hotel in the South. It was torn down in 1917, and a great pity it was, too. It should have been preserved, for it was a beautiful building. I remember so well how a group of us tried to save it from destruction and how we were laughed at for our pains. It was a fascinating old building with its winding stair, a magnificent dome, its frescoes; it was all so ornate, and such a complete outgrowth of its period.* [7]

Beginning in the late 19th century, and continuing through the first half of the 20th century, artists and photographers recognized the unique and increasingly endangered nature of the city and its diverse populations, using them as inspiration for their works. These now serve as documents of an older way of life. A number of these works, including *Uptown Street* by Lulu King Saxon, *Portrait of John L. Sullivan* by Achille Peretti, *Old Gentilly Road* by Andres Molinary, *French Market, New Orleans* by Robert Grafton, *French Quarter Street Scene* by William Woodward and *Iris Field Near Newcomb Greenhouse* by Ellsworth Woodward, are now included in the collection of The Ogden Museum of Southern Art.

After World War II, the pace of life in New Orleans accelerated, as did the rate of loss for historic structures and neighborhoods, although not as rapidly as in many parts of the nation. Artists, writers and musicians continued to live and work in the French Quarter. John McCrady maintained a studio and an art school in the French Quarter, as reflected in a self-portrait of the artist working in his studio in *The Parade*, which also featured an historic Mardi Gras parade moving through the district. Noel Rockmore, recognized as a painter active in the life and culture of the French Quarter, created an historic series of portraits of Preservation Hall musicians, such as *Bill Matthews, Preservation Hall* and *Billie and DeDe Pierce, Preservation Hall*, also featured in The Ogden Museum collection.

Since the 1960s and 1970s, as the forces of preservation and "progress" in New Orleans have engaged in ongoing battles, many landmarks have disappeared, yet many have been preserved. The city, as in the past, continues to evolve. For example, the 1984 World's Fair preserved much of the endangered warehouse district, creating the foundation for the 21st century's flourishing Warehouse Arts District, including its Museum District. In this area, projects such as The Ogden Museum of Southern Art have combined new

▲ Lulu King Saxon's large-scale landscape *Uptown Street* depicts Magazine Street in its more agrarian days of the 1890s. *(Ogden Museum Permanent Collection)*

construction (Stephen Goldring Hall, 2003) with the preservation of a landmark structure (Henry Hobson Richardson's Howard Memorial Library of 1889, now known as the Patrick F. Taylor Library). Nearby, museums and cultural institutions including the Contemporary Arts Center, the National D-Day Museum, the Louisiana Children's Museum and the Louisiana ArtWorks have incorporated new or adaptive reuse projects with extensive historic preservation endeavors.

The Cabildo, one of the iconic symbols of historic Jackson Square, which was heavily damaged by a disastrous fire in 1988, was restored and hosted celebrations for the bicentennial of the Louisiana Purchase in 2003. Next door, historic St. Louis Cathedral has undergone extensive exterior renovations. Nearby, after years of preservation and adaptive reuse planning, the Supreme Court Building reopened in 2004. Not far away, on Canal Street, the Customs House, where original construction was supervised by Thomas Wharton in the 1850s, is undergoing major restoration and conversion to serve as a new museum complex operated by the Audubon Nature Institute.

As this book clearly indicates, and as a tour of the parking lots of downtown and the surrounding districts suggests, much has been lost in New Orleans. While much of the city's historic fabric remains, many of its most important sites have been sacrificed. Current preservation projects across the city seem to suggest an enhanced awareness and appreciation of the city's unique culture and history. Projects such as this book, planned and designed by Phillip Collier with text by Jim Rapier and Mary Beth Romig, supported by The Goldring Family Foundation and The Ogden Museum of Southern Art, remind us of our own place, and our own responsibilities, within the larger continuum of New Orleans history.

J. Richard Gruber, Ph.D.

▲ William Woodward and his brother, Ellsworth, often depicted the architectural and artistic value of New Orleans' Vieux Carré, which they considered endangered, as in *French Quarter Street Scene*, rendered by William in 1909. *(Ogden Museum Permanent Collection)*

[1] Mary Herczog, *Frommer's New Orleans 2005* (Hoboken, N.J.: Wiley Publishing Inc., 2004), 1. [2] Roy Blount Jr., *Feet on the Street, Rambles Around New Orleans* (New York: Crown Publishing Group, 2005), 17. [3] Samuel Wilson, Jr., Patricia Brady and Lynn D. Adams, editors, *Queen of the South, New Orleans, 1853-1863: The Journal of Thomas K. Wharton* (New Orleans: The Historic New Orleans Collection and The New York Public Library, 1999), 77. [4] Mark Twain, *Life on the Mississippi*, in Judy Long, editor, *Literary New Orleans* (Athens, Hill Street Press, 1999), 40. [5] Louis Armstrong, *Satchmo: My Life in New Orleans* in *Literary New Orleans*, 150. [6] Sherwood Anderson, "New Orleans, the Double Dealer and the Modern Movement in America," in *Literary New Orleans*, 86. [7] Lyle Saxon, *Fabulous New Orleans* (New Orleans, Robert L. Crager & Company, 1954), 272.

Pg. 2 Vieux Carre Map, from *The Tourist in New Orleans*, a guidebook, published by Mrs. A. Sniderman, © Irma Herndon; **Pg. 5** Lover's Lane, Audubon Park, courtesy of The Historic New Orleans Collection; **Pg. 6-7** Canal Street & Saenger Theatre, photograph by C. F. Weber, courtesy of Bergeron Gallery; **Pg. 8-9** Canal Street at Night in Rain, photograph by C. F. Weber, courtesy of Bergeron Gallery; **Pg. 10** Café Exile, illustration courtesy of The Historic New Orleans Collection; **Pg. 13** Record album *PETE FOUNTAIN At The BATEAUX LOUNGE,* courtesy of Pete Fountain; **Pg. 14** Cockeyed Circus photograph by James K. Collier, courtesy of Phillip Collier; **Pg. 14** Old Absinthe House, courtesy of The Historic New Orleans Collection; **Pg 15** Blue Room, Roosevelt Hotel, New Orleans, Louisiana, courtesy of The Fairmont Hotel New Orleans; **Pg. 15** Photograph Courtesy of Phillip Collier; **Pg. 16** S. S. Admiral (postcard), St. Louis, Missouri; **Pg. 16** Poster with Rosy's logo, courtesy of Milton Glaser, artist; **Pg. 18** William Woodward, *St. Louis Hotel*, 1904, gift of the Roger Houston Ogden Collection, © 1913 Eleanor Woodward Westfeldt, courtesy of The Ogden Museum of Southern Art; **Pg. 19** Thomas Sully, *Portrait of Mrs. Robb and Her Three Children*, 1844, gift of the Roger Houston Ogden Collection, courtesy of The Ogden Museum of Southern Art; **Pg. 20** Louis Armstrong, courtesy of The Louisiana State Museum; **Pg. 21** *St. Charles Hotel*, 1910, gift of the Roger Houston Ogden Collection, courtesy of The Ogden Museum of Southern Art; **Pg. 22** Lulu King Saxon, *Uptown Street*, 1890, gift of the Roger Houston Ogden Collection, courtesy of The Ogden Museum of Southern Art; **Pg. 23** William Woodward, *French Quarter Street Scene*, 1909, gift of the Roger Houston Ogden Collection, courtesy of Ogden Museum of Southern Art; **Pg. 24** *Crescent City Jockey Club*, gift of the Roger Houston Ogden Collection, Library of Congress, Prints & Photographs Division, Detroit Publishing Company, Collection, courtesy of The Ogden Museum of Southern Art

Horses finish the handicap at the Crescent City Jockey Club, 1906. The Crescent City Jockey Club was founded in 1892, and ran the Fair Grounds until 1908, when the Louisiana Legislature abolished the sport. By 1915 racing was legal again. In 1918, this grandstand burned to the ground and was replaced in three days by the grandstand from the former City Park Race Track. *(Ogden Museum Permanent Collection)*

YOU'LL LINGER THERE

EATING, DRINKING, AND SLEEPING IN NEW ORLEANS

(Previous Page) The second St. Charles Hotel came to a blazing end in 1894.

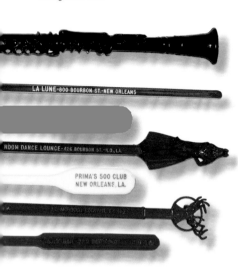

▲ Classic swizzle sticks, varying in style, harken back to the lounges and nightclubs where patrons enjoyed the Bourbon Street nightlife – and a few cocktails – including clarinetist Pete Fountain's Lounge, La Lune, Tony Bacino's, The Dream Room Dance Lounge, Prima's 500 Club, The El Morocco Cocktail Lounge and the Sho Bar.

I n the antebellum era, when New Orleans was called the "Queen of the South," it became one of the nation's largest and most prosperous cities. Many factors influenced New Orleans's development as a commercial and trade center during this period, beginning with the Louisiana Purchase, in 1803, and the arrival, in 1812, of Robert Fulton's paddle wheeler, the *New Orleans*, marking the beginning of the steamboat era on the Mississippi River. In 1812, Louisiana was admitted to statehood, and three years later the Battle of New Orleans opened the city's port and the Mississippi River to international trade. It was the era of King Cotton and the sugar cane industry, built upon plantation systems and slave labor, bringing cotton, sugar and many diverse people to, and through, the Crescent City.

New Orleans, founded in 1718, developed under French and Spanish rule but its early architecture was largely destroyed in the great fires of 1788 and 1794. While the old city was rebuilt by the Spanish, the dominant historic architecture of the city appeared during its antebellum era. As the city developed new levels of wealth and fashionable tastes, this became evident in its competing Creole and American districts, including the Garden District and Esplanade Avenue.

Two of the nation's most elegant hotels, designed when the hotel as a building type was being developed across America, opened in New Orleans on competing sides of the Canal Street neutral ground. The Creole's City Exchange (St. Louis) Hotel, designed by J. N. B. de Pouilly, built in 1836, was located in the French Quarter. The St. Charles Exchange Hotel, designed in the Greek Revival style by James Gallier and

▼ By 1912, the once grand St. Louis Hotel had become a run-down haven for livestock and bats.

26

completed in 1842, served as the cultural center of the American district. Here, while visitors and the city's elite classes dined and drank in splendor, slave auctions often occurred in each hotel's rotunda, reflecting other realities in the Deep South. The St. Charles, rebuilt three times, was adjoined by similar institutions including the Verandah Hotel, noted for its ironwork gallery, designed in 1836 by James and Charles Dakin.

These hotels offered refined restaurants and bars, and over time the city was recognized increasingly for its fine food and distilled spirits. The fusion of the city's diverse cultures changed the tastes of millions of visitors. Creole and other restaurant traditions originated at establishments like Antoine's, Arnaud's and Galatoire's. Other restaurants, including Bégué's, Maylie's, Kolb's, Solari's and Lenfant's, expanded the city's traditions and reputation over the years.

The 19th century tradition of grand hotels continued at the Grunewald Hotel, which served as the home of a popular club called the "Cave." Later, the Roosevelt Hotel, which incorporated the older Grunewald Hotel, was recognized as one of the South's great 20th century hotels. After entering its lobby, visitors could go to the famous "Blue Room," known for its music and live radio broadcasts, dance in the Fountain Lounge, or stop in the historic Sazerac Bar, where they could drink a Sazerac and see the murals of New Orleans artist Paul Ninas. The murals are preserved today in the renamed Fairmont Hotel.

Bars, saloons and drinking establishments were located in neighborhoods across the city. By 1898, there were reportedly more than 800 saloons in the city. Bourbon Street may be the best known location for drinking in the city, amplified by its reputation as a music and adult entertainment center. Musicians and performers of all types have been associated with the street over the years, including those like Blaze Starr, the Oyster Girl, Lilly Christine the Cat Girl and others who made the stages of Bourbon Street clubs famous.

Rampart Street was another important cultural district, continuing into the Tremé neighborhood, with its many clubs, bars and restaurants, where many of the city's most significant musical traditions were nurtured. Here you found the Gypsy Tea Room, Economy Hall (the Economy and Mutual Aid Association), the Astoria Hotel and Ball Room, the Pythian Temple and clubs such as the Red Onion and Parisian Garden. Young Louis Armstrong knew these streets, and was encouraged by Louis Karnofsky and his family, illustrating the unique social and racial interaction evident in the city. Nearby Congo Square served as a reminder, as it does today, of the historic roots of the musical traditions which evolved here.

The Roosevelt Hotel—New Orleans

▲ During its reign as The Roosevelt Hotel, originally the Grunewald Hotel, the property continued to flourish. Its owner and manager, Seymour Weiss, befriended Huey P. Long, who established his campaign headquarters for Governor of Louisiana in the hotel. Long moved in shortly after winning the election, spending so much time there that Louisiana lore says he built a 50-mile highway – Airline – directly from Baton Rouge, the state's capital, to the hotel's door. The Roosevelt bore that name until 1965, when new management assumed the property, renaming it the Fairmont New Orleans.

▶ The great storm of 1915 caused irreparable damage to the once grand St. Louis Hotel, as shown in this image of its landmark dome taken after the hurricane. The owners demolished the property soon after.

NEW ORLEANS, La. Old St. Louis Hotel.

ST. LOUIS HOTEL

Designed by French architect J. N. B. de Pouilly and opened in 1836, the St. Louis Hotel, also known as the City Exchange, stretched a block long on St. Louis Street and was considered the most elegant hotel in the French Quarter's Creole sector. Its features included an elegant ballroom and a beautiful circular stairway. Despite its size, it only accommodated 200 guests. Guests could enter by way of Exchange Alley and walk to the landmark domed rotunda. Sixty-five feet in diameter and 88 feet tall, it was in this rotunda where auctions for property, including slaves, were conducted. It was also during this time period that the hotel's proprietors, specifically M. Philippe Alvarez, manager of the St. Louis Bar, introduced the concept of "free lunch." As auctioneering took place generally between the hours of noon and 3:00 p.m., serving free lunch kept the businessmen in the hotel, an idea that would spread throughout the United States. During the Civil War years the hotel began its decline. Despite the owners' efforts to revitalize the property, it never returned to its former grandeur. It was used by the Louisiana Legislature from 1874 to 1882, and by 1903 was in ramshackle condition. The Royal Orleans Hotel now welcomes guests where the St. Louis Hotel once stood.

ST. CHARLES HOTEL I *Luxurious and opulent, the James Gallier Sr. designed St. Charles Hotel, the first of three properties to bear that name in the same location, was originally called the St. Charles Exchange Hotel. Built in response to the St. Louis Hotel, and equally as grand, it was a popular destination in the American section of town accommodating 1,000 guests. Opened in 1842, the hotel, with its tall Corinthian columns, faced St. Charles Avenue, and cost $750,000 to build, including furnishings. Its dome, 46 feet in diameter and rising to a height of 185 feet, could be seen for miles. The hotel included shops, an octagonal barroom and elegant ballroom. After nine years, the original St. Charles Hotel was destroyed by fire.*

The six-story St. Charles Hotel was the tallest building in New Orleans and provided guests panoramic views of the city. This daguerreotype by Thomas Easterly is the only photograph of the first St. Charles Hotel known to exist.

Like its predecessor, the second St. Charles Hotel was a grand structure in the second block of St. Charles Avenue, as viewed from Canal Street.

ST. CHARLES HOTEL II

In 1853, a second St. Charles Hotel rose from the charred wreckage of the first. Designed by Isaiah Rogers and George Purvis, it was located on the same site, and resembled its predecessor, but without a dome. It also catered to a lavish lifestyle, but with improvements. The second St. Charles Hotel had more chandeliers than the first and featured hot and cold running water in the baths located on the ground floor. Following the Civil War, the management offered free accommodations to returning Confederate soldiers. Lasting longer than its predecessor, the hotel burned in 1894. The fire was so extensive that only the pediment and columns remained.

The skylights in the Palm Gardens Lounge of the third St. Charles Hotel created a conservatory-like environment for patrons at the turn of the century.

ST. CHARLES HOTEL III *After the second St. Charles Hotel burned, a third one was built on the same location, opening in 1896. Designed by Thomas Sully in the Italian-Renaissance style, it featured a grand staircase in its lobby. Keeping with tradition, the third St. Charles Hotel served guests in a first-class manner, playing host to balls and formal gatherings. This hotel lasted longer than the previous ones, and was demolished in 1974 to the dismay of many local citizens. At the time of its demolition it was the Sheraton-St. Charles Hotel. Today the location is the site of an office building towering 52 floors.*

◄ Hypolite Bégué, who acted as the restaurant's maître d' and business manager, took pleasure in demonstrating to customers the proper way of peeling crawfish, one of the popular items served at Madame Bégué's.

▶ Madame Bégué's location in the French Quarter, at Madison and Decatur — then Old Levée — Streets near Jackson Square, was also known as Little Italy at the turn of the century.

MADAME BÉGUÉ'S

Located on Decatur Street across from the French Market, the restaurant known as Bégué's was originally called the Coffee House when it was operated by Louis Dutrey and his German immigrant wife, Elizabeth. Their eatery was popular with the butchers working in the market, who after rising long before dawn, were hungry for a second breakfast at midday. Following her husband's death, Elizabeth kept the business going, joined by a French butcher, Hypolite Bégué, who gave up his trade to serve as bartender. The couple married, changing the restaurant to Madame Bégué's, but while the name changed, the tradition of the second breakfast remained, gaining international fame during the 1884-85 World's Industrial and Cotton Centennial Exposition, held in New Orleans. Bégué's opened at 11:00 a.m. and served breakfast only until 3:00 p.m., a forerunner to what is commonly called "brunch" today. Her extensive meals – one included 50 items plus wine for $1 – were prepared on a cast-iron, wood-burning stove. Bégué's closed in 1917, and is now Tujaque's Restaurant.

Located in the Faubourg Tremé on the edge of the French Quarter in what is now Louis Armstrong Park, Congo Square, in the 19th century, was a gathering place on Sundays for enslaved Africans and free people of color, where they conducted business and socialized. They would sing and dance, performing the bamboula and the calinda, an African line dance. These dances, intermingled with Caribbean and European musical traditions, would form one of the roots of jazz music, said to have its origins in Congo Square.

FAUBOURG TREMÉ

Bound by Rampart, Canal, St. Bernard and Broad Streets, the Tremé area is an historic neighborhood that has been home to Native Americans, European immigrants and free people of color. It has also been referred to as "America's Oldest Black Neighborhood." It was a social gathering place for African-Americans, especially in the late 1800s, when it began to flourish. One of the great social spots was the Gypsy Tea Room, where patrons could hear the early sounds of jazz from the area's greats such as George Lewis, Chris Kelly, Jimmy Noone and Henry Ragas.

The Jones and Collins Astoria Hot Eight Orchestra, the hotel house band, put the Astoria Hotel and Ballroom in the limelight with their 1929 Victor recording of the *Astoria Strut*.

RAMPART STREET

The African-American community was pivotal to the growth of commercial activity, social halls and music establishments in the South Rampart area. It was one of the first African-American shopping areas in New Orleans. Among the many establishments on Rampart Street were the Tick Tock Tavern, the Iroquois Theater and Karnofsky Store and residence. The Karnofsky family offered a young Louis Armstrong a job and lodging, and proved influential in his future as a musician. People lived in this area as well, including notable residents Armstrong and Jelly Roll Morton. Jazz in the early 1900s flourished in such establishments as the Red Onion, the Parisian Garden, the Pythian Temple building and the Astoria Hotel and Ballroom. An offshoot of Rampart Street was Chinatown, occupied by Asian immigrant families seeking employment in the city. Today that area is the city's Medical Complex. Another part of the South Rampart area known as "Back O' Town," which was near present day City Hall, was home to gambling houses, brothels, saloons and theaters. Very little remains of what was once this thriving part of the city.

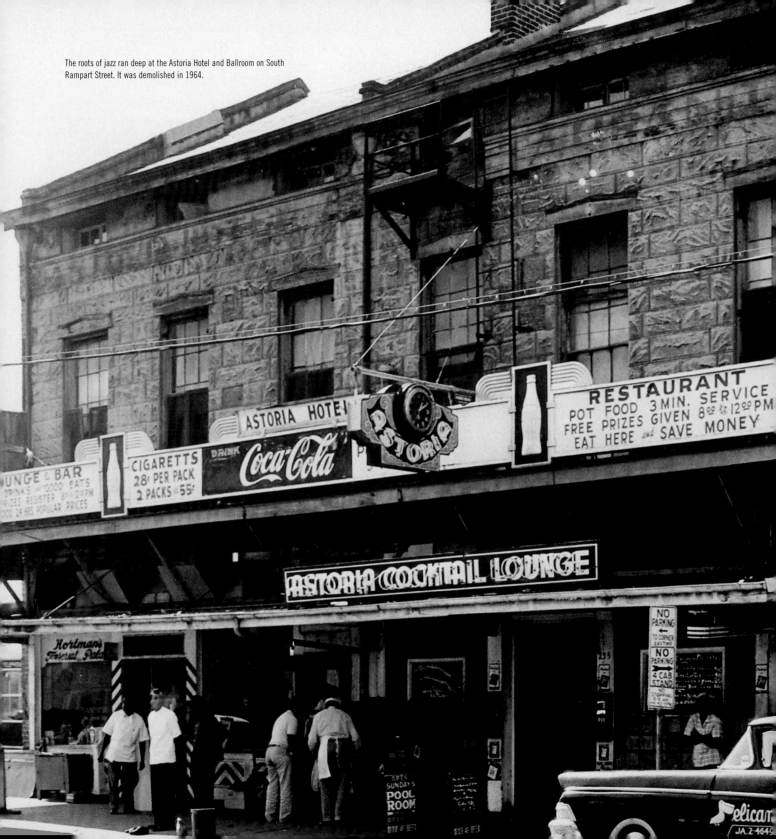

The roots of jazz ran deep at the Astoria Hotel and Ballroom on South Rampart Street. It was demolished in 1964.

SOLARI'S *Located on the corner of Royal and Iberville, Solari's, founded in 1864, was considered the pre-eminent Creole grocery widely known for its gourmet delicacies. It catered to locals and shipped nationwide. Solari's inventory included rare liquors, cooked hams, choice meats, out-of-season vegetables and a candy kitchen featuring cookies and candies imported from Europe. New Orleanians knew it as a popular spot for delicious lunches served at its large lunch counter and soda fountain that spanned the store's center. Solari's closed in the early 1960s, and today is the site of a parking garage.*

Solari's branded its own line of products, such as tea, which it sold to locals or shipped to out-of-town customers.

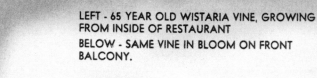

LEFT - 65 YEAR OLD WISTARIA VINE, GROWING FROM INSIDE OF RESTAURANT

BELOW - SAME VINE IN BLOOM ON FRONT BALCONY.

Maylie's Restaurant

CORNER POYDRAS & DRYADES STREETS
NEW ORLEANS, LA. - EST. 1876

MAYLIE'S

In 1876, Bernard Maylie and Hypolite Esparbe opened an eatery that catered to the butchers of the Poydras Marke Maylie's served only men until 1925. A unique feature of the restaurant was a large wisteria vine whose trunk, more than a foot in diameter, vaulte upward through the dining room and out onto the balcony. Maylie's closed in 1986 and is the present site of Smith and Wollensky's steakhouse.

The Grunewald Hotel, New Orleans, La.

THE FAMOUS CAVE UNDER THIS BUILDING.

THE GRUNEWALD

Louis Grunewald opened his six-story hotel known as "The Pride of the South" on Baronne Street in 1893. A 14-story annex was added in 1908. With its marbled staircase, statues in the lobby, a ladies' tearoom and a small theater for the hotel's orchestra, the Grunewald quickly grew in popularity. Grunewald died in 1915, and his son took over the hotel's operations before selling it in 1923, when it was renamed the Roosevelt, honoring the nation's 26th President, Theodore. Today, the grand hotel is known as the Fairmont.

◀ An ingenious use of the building, cement and plaster produced the unforgettable atmosphere of the Cave in the basement of the Grunewald Hotel. The subterranean supper club resembled the Mammoth Caves in Kentucky, with such features as waterfalls and streams, and stalagmites and stalactites that covered the pipes and beams. The Cave was the site of lavish musical revues in the Ziegfeld tradition, Dixieland bands and some of the nation's finest stars of the time. It welcomed patrons until the 1930s, and today houses the laundry of the Fairmont Hotel.

While the decorative features were blue, over the decades the Blue Room underwent a series of renovations. A mainstay, however, was the Leon Kelner Orchestra, the house band for the elegant club.

BLUE ROOM, THE ROOSEVELT, NEW ORLEANS, LOUISIA

BLUE ROOM *On New Year's Eve, 1935, the Roosevelt Hotel opened the Blue Room and so began a long run of elegant dining, dancing and top-notch showmanship. Legends such as Frank Sinatra, Tony Bennett, Jack Benny, Cab Calloway, Ray Charles, Debbie Reynolds, Jimmy Durante, Marlene Dietrich and Tina Turner played the room over the decades. Big name bands including Glenn Miller, the Dorsey Brothers, Guy Lombardo and Sammy Kaye also graced the stage. WWL-Radio moved to the Roosevelt for a time and until 1969 broadcast live nightly from the Blue Room, reaching American audiences with its powerful watts, including the Armed Forces during World War II. The Blue Room still exists in the hotel now known as the Fairmont, but is only used for private receptions.*

On a visit to Leon Prima's 500 Club on Bourbon Street in the 1940s and 50s, entertainment included vaudeville acts, comedians and burlesque.

BOURBON STREET *Long before the present-day t-shirt shops and strip clubs dotted the sidewalks, Bourbon Street, one of the first thoroughfares in the city, was one of the most fashionable residential streets in the Vieux Carré. In the 1920s, residences gave way to nightlife. From the 1930s to the 60s, Bourbon Street was noted for its concentration of clubs, including the Silver Slipper, the Famous Door, Pier 600 and Al Hirt's Club. Clarinetist Pete Fountain also operated his popular nightclub on Bourbon Street. At that time, a night on the town meant dressing up and taking in shows that featured jazz, exotic dancers, singers, comics, contortionists and burlesque performers such as Lilly Christine the Cat Girl.*

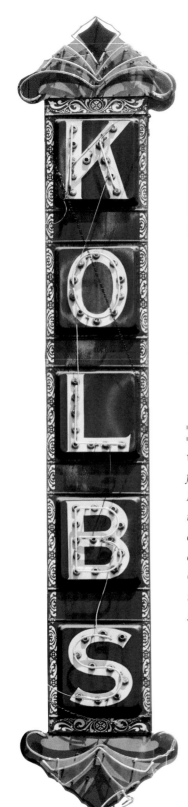

KOLB'S — ST. CHARLES NEAR CANAL — NEW ORLEANS

"The Restaurant With An Individuality"

KOLB'S — ST. CHARLES NEAR CANAL — NEW ORLEANS

"The Restaurant With An Individuality"

KOLB'S *A wrought-iron façade, a large vertical sign marking the entrance, belt-driven ceiling fans from the 1884-85 World's Industrial and Cotton Centennial Exposition held in New Orleans and beer steins decorating the walls were the trademarks of Kolb's Restaurant. Located on St. Charles Avenue, in the first block off of Canal Street, it opened in 1899 and gave locals a taste of schnitzel and other German dishes. Kolb's closed in 1994, but while the building is empty, the trademark wrought-iron balconies and famous sign still remain.*

LENFANT'S

The Lenfant family operated a popular drive-in restaurant, Lenfant's, in a Streamline Moderne structure, known for its unique architecture and the lobster dressed as a waiter on its exterior sign. Located on Canal Boulevard near the cemeteries in the neighborhood called Lakeview, patrons could dine in their cars in its oyster-shell parking lot, or eat inside near the huge bar. A pick-up window in the rear allowed customers to take their meals home. Lenfant's closed in the 1970s, and owners tried to make a comeback with the property as a disco in the 80s. It is now the site of All Faiths Funeral Home.

Pg. 25 An Historic Hotel: Burning of the St. Charles Hotel, New Orleans, Louisiana, on April 30, 1894, *The Illustrated Weekly*, Vol. XV, No. 20, © 1984 Lorillard Spencer; **Pg. 26** Swizzle Sticks, Photograph by C. F. Weber, courtesy of Bergeron Gallery; **Pg. 26** Demolition of the St. Louis Hotel Dome, courtesy of the New Orleans Public Library; **Pg. 27** The Roosevelt Hotel, New Orleans (postcard), courtesy of The Fairmont Hotel New Orleans; **Pg. 27** Roosevelt Hotel luggage tag, courtesy of Phillip Collier; **Pg. 28** Old St. Louis Hotel (postcard), New Orleans, Louisiana, courtesy of The Historic New Orleans Collection; **Pg. 29** St. Louis Hotel dome, interior, courtesy of The Historic New Orleans Collection; **Pg. 30** St. Charles Hotel I, courtesy of The Historic New Orleans Collection; **Pg. 31** Thomas M. Easterly, St. Charles Hotel, New Orleans, ca. 1847, courtesy of The Missouri Historical Society; **Pg. 32** Photograph of St. Charles Hotel II, from the George Francois Mugnier Photograph Collection, courtesy of The Historic New Orleans Collection **Pg. 33** Interior of St. Charles Hotel II, *Illustrated Newspaper*, Frank Leslie, December 2, 1876; **Pg. 34** The St. Charles Hotel III, New Orleans, Louisiana, C. B. Mason; **Pg. 35** Palm Gardens, The St. Charles Hotel III, courtesy of New Orleans Public Library; **Pg. 36** Photograph of Hypolite Bégué, Frank B. Moore Collection, Earl K. Long Library, University of New Orleans; **Pg. 37** Madame Bégué's Famous Breakfast House (postcard), 200 Years Old, New Orleans, Louisiana, 1908 © C. B. Mason, courtesy of The Historic New Orleans Collection; **Pg. 38** Congo Square, Sketch by Edward W. Kemble for "Creole Slave Songs" by George W. Cable, *Century Magazine*, April 1886; **Pg. 39** Gypsy Tea Room, courtesy of The Historic New Orleans Collection; **Pg. 40** Astoria Strut record, photograph by Mike Terranova, courtesy of The Louisiana State Museum; **Pg. 41** Astoria Cocktail Lounge, courtesy of The Historic New Orleans Collection; **Pg. 42** Solari's tea label, courtesy of Phillip Collier; **Pg. 42** Solari's, New Orleans, courtesy of The Historic New Orleans Collection; **Pg. 43** Maylie's Restaurant, New Orleans, Louisiana, Alphonse Goldsmith, courtesy of The Historic New Orleans Collection; **Pg. 44** The Cave (interior) courtesy of The Historic New Orleans Collection; **Pg. 45** The Grunewald Hotel, New Orleans, Louisiana, courtesy of The Historic New Orleans Collection; **Pg. 45** Soup Plate Crystal Cave, the Grunewald, photograph by Joe Bergeron, courtesy of Al Kleindienst; **Pg. 46** Roosevelt Hotel ash tray, photograph by Mike Terranova, courtesy of The Fairmont Hotel New Orleans; **Pg. 47** Blue Room (postcard), The Roosevelt, New Orleans, Louisiana, courtesy of The Fairmont Hotel New Orleans; **Pg. 47** Blue Room coaster, photograph by Mike Terranova, courtesy of Al Kleindienst; **Pg. 48** Fabulous Fannie, photograph by Bob Coke, courtesy of Bergeron Gallery; **Pg. 49** Bourbon Street, photograph by C. F. Weber, courtesy of Bergeron Gallery; **Pg. 50** Kolb's Restaurant sign, photograph by Mike Terranova; **Pg. 50** Kolb's Restaurant – St. Charles, near Canal Street – New Orleans (postcard), Thomas Dune Co., Inc.; **Pg. 50** Kolb's Restaurant – St. Charles, near Canal Street – New Orleans, Louisiana, courtesy of The Historic New Orleans Collection; **Pg. 51** Kolb's plate, photograph by Mike Terranova, courtesy of Al Kleindienst; **Pg. 52-53** Lenfant's Restaurant, photograph by C. F. Weber, courtesy of Bergeron Gallery; **Pg. 54** Old Absinthe House Bar sign, photograph by Mike Terranova

The Old Absinthe Bar at 400 Bourbon Street opened after Prohibition. Cousin to the Old Absinthe House, it featured the latter's original cypress bar, green marble absinthe fountains and charm. The bar closed in 1998, and the building was remodeled and is today a daiquiri shop. The original bar and fountain was returned to The Old Absinthe House. The only thing that remains of the original Old Absinthe House Bar is the sign that hangs high above the street.

JINGLE, JANGLE, JINGLE

BUSINESS IN NEW ORLEANS

(Previous Page) Called "The Broadway of the South," Canal Street was built 171-feet wide with plans to accommodate a canal that was never realized. It was home to popular department stores and shops. Today, most of the original structures from this postcard detail still exist.

▲ The markets throughout the city in the 1800s were common places for vendors to sell their wares, as the Choctaw selling filé for gumbo in the French Market, depicted in this illustration.

▲ At one time, New Orleans ranked among the world's greatest banana ports, with more than 700 ships arriving each year loaded with 25,000 – 50,000 bunches of bananas.

he Mississippi River and the port made new business opportunities and new wealth possible in New Orleans. Initially, King Cotton ruled the rivers and the plantations of Louisiana, Mississippi and the Deep South. Here in New Orleans, he had his own palace and throne room, the Cotton Exchange. In 1883, a new home for the Cotton Exchange opened, adorned with a fountain, frescoes and a visitor's gallery. And, as sugar cane plantations flourished, and sugar was shipped with greater frequency through the port, an impressive Sugar Exchange building opened in the city as well.

New Orleans developed a reputation as a major banking and financial center during the antebellum era. The United States Mint opened here in a Greek revival building designed by William Strickland, and coins were minted then and during the era of the Confederacy. One of the most prominent early banks in the city was the Citizens' Bank, located in the French Quarter. Later, during the late 19th and early 20th centuries, a series of notable New Orleans banking institutions developed, including the Whitney and Hibernia banks, located in the American sector, now known as the Central Business District.

After the Civil War, when the agricultural and economic structure of the South changed, the port assumed a new importance. Coffee, a significant commodity in a city recognized for its coffee houses, became increasingly important. The diverse range of coffee products and brands associated with the city reflect coffee's historic and continuing importance here. Bananas also became a major trade commodity after the Civil War, when New Orleans business families made new connections to Central America. Later, the United Fruit Company took over these local businesses and used New Orleans as a principle port, enhancing the city's reputation then as the gateway to Latin America.

Fresh food and produce came into the city in many ways – over unpaved rural roads and city streets, across the lake and through the canal system, through the city's port and eventually on railroads, and from surrounding agricultural areas – supplying the city's markets, restaurants and commercial establishments. New Orleans residents were often found "making market" or "making groceries" in places like the French Market, the Poydras Market and the St. Roch Market.

Equally popular were the many vendors who roamed the streets, bringing fresh produce and eclectic products through the neighborhoods, sounding out their wares with unique calls, including the blackberry woman, the praline ladies, the vegetable peddlers, the basket ladies and the clothespole man. Others roamed the streets on horse or mule-drawn wagons, including the milkman, the bottle man, the waffle man and those selling fuel for fires and lights.

The city's primary shopping district was located in the French Quarter along Royal and Chartres streets before it moved to Canal Street. New Orleans became recognized as an urban center for shopping and retail activities, and Canal Street served as the hub for these activities. Major department stores, including the D. H. Holmes store and Maison Blanche, were founded here and developed on Canal Street, becoming iconic parts of the city's life. Other department stores followed, including Godchaux's, Kreeger's, Gus Mayer's and the Krauss store.

Dryades Street also developed as a prominent shopping neighborhood, reflecting a complex mixture of races, religions and nationalities. Dryades Street became a center for African-American, Jewish and Italian families, as well as diverse businesses including Kaufman's Department Store, the Keystone Insurance Company, children's clothing and shoe stores, drug stores and groceries. In this neighborhood the Dryades Street YMCA, St. John the Baptist Church and the Congregation Beth Israel and Congregation Anshe Sfard Synagogues served as social and religious centers.

New business traditions and innovations were established along Canal Street and across the city. Katz and Besthoff introduced a chain of drug stores, beginning on Canal Street in 1905, notable for its early use of electric lighting in its signage. In time, K&B's popular soda fountains and purple signs evolved into an iconic part of the city's landscape. The Schwegmann's chain of grocery stores served as another retail icon, emerging as an innovative chain of modern supermarkets, expanding as the city grew and reflecting the post-war interest in convenience, competitive pricing and accessibility by automobile.

A different type of innovation was evident in the products built by Andrew Higgins and his boat company. Modifying a boat originally designed for use in the swamps of Louisiana for military purposes, the Higgins boat, or LCVP, played a central role in the D-Day invasion at Normandy. Higgins was an innovator and visionary, one Dwight D. Eisenhower called "the man who won the war." His plants spread across the city and in City Park, along Bayou St. John and near the lakefront area, where his boats were launched and tested. The Higgins plants were innovative for their hiring practices in the segregated South as well, employing men and women of diverse races, paying them equally.

▲ Godchaux's Department Store on Canal Street was an exclusive clothing store for men and women that was founded in 1840 and closed in 1985. This medal celebrates the store's centennial.

▶ Prefixes of telephone numbers indicated to New Orleanians the area of town they lived in, such as HUnter, MAgnolia, RAymond and GAlvez, as shown on the ink blotter advertising a neighborhood K&B drugstore.

The Citizens' Bank building, with its columns facing Toulouse Street, was one of the largest state-chartered banks in America before falling into disrepair.

CITIZENS' BANK *Chartered by the State Legislature in 1833, the Greek-Revival style Citizens' Bank was designed by J. N. B. dePouilly and located on Toulouse Street between Royal and Chartres Streets. The structure was grand, as most banks of the day were, and featured vaulted ceilings with paintings rendered by Dominico Canova, who had come to New Orleans to paint the ceilings of the nearby St. Louis Hotel and who would become one of the city's most sought-after artists. The bank served both French and English- speaking customers, printing $10 bills with English on one side and French on the other. The French word for 10 is "DIX," and it wasn't long before English-speaking tongues were mispronouncing the word "Dixies." The term evolved to "Dixieland," coming to mean more than New Orleans, applying to the entire South, where $10 bills were plentiful. After the Civil War, the building's fortunes declined with those of the French Quarter, and by 1884 was a crumbling ruin.*

The New Orleans Mint was the only one in America to have served both as a U.S. and Confederate Mint. Mexican currency was also minted at this site.

▶ New Orleans-minted coins were marked with a small "o" imprinted on the reverse side.

THE MINT *Located at Esplanade Avenue and the Mississippi River, the New Orleans Mint left its impression on the economy, operating in the Neo-classical style building designed by William Strickland and built in 1835. Prior to 1835, Fort St. Charles occupied the site and was where Andrew Jackson reviewed his troops before the Battle of New Orleans. The Mint was constructed, and numerous denominations of coins were manufactured, including double eagles, eagles and half eagles in gold, and dollars, halves, quarters, dimes, half-dimes and three-cent pieces in silver. Confederate coinage was also produced during the Civil War. The Mint ceased operations in 1909 and was decommissioned in 1911. The machinery was transferred to the main U.S. Mint facility in Philadelphia. The building then served as an assay office, Federal prison and Coast Guard storage facility. Today it is a branch of the Louisiana State Museum.*

THE COTTON EXCHANGE

Cotton was king by the mid-1830s, with the port of New Orleans shipping half a million bales of cotton, earning the city the reputation as the cotton capital of the world. The Cotton Exchange was founded in 1871 by cotton merchants and brokers to promote trade and regulate prices. The Exchange constructed its own building on Carondolet and Gravier in 1883, designed by H. Wolters. The ornate monument to cotton was the first commercial structure in New Orleans to include a cellar, an architectural innovation for the time in the city due to the low water table, made possible by improvements in building techniques. The Wolters building was replaced in the 1920s by a new building that continued to serve as the Cotton Exchange. That building still stands today and serves as the Cotton Exchange Hotel.

7024. COTTON EXCHANGE. NEW ORLEANS. LA.

COPYRIGHT 1903, BY DETROIT PHOTOGRAPHIC CO.

▶ Author Mark Twain once described the Cotton Exchange as, "Massive, substantial, full of architectural graces." This palace of commerce was erected at a cost of $400,000 and included frescoes depicting Louisiana scenes and a fountain, around which cotton futures were sold.

Going to market on the dirt thoroughfare *Old Gentilly Road* was depicted by artist Andres Molinary in 1890. It was one of many routes vendors from outlying areas traveled to sell produce and supplies in New Orleans markets. *(Ogden Museum Permanent Collection)*

▸ Among the city's public markets, the Tremé Market offered residents of the neighborhood a place to shop.

PUBLIC MARKETS

From New Orleans' earliest days, open-air markets, pre-cursors to neighborhood grocery stores, were popular sites offering an immense variety of produce, meats, fish and other goods to shoppers. Because the markets were considered too rough for ladies, it was a Creole tradition for gentlemen to do the marketing for their households, where the options were limitless to customers. Vendors came from far and near, with Irish, German, Italian, French, Hispanic, African-American, Creole and American sectors supplying goods. Some crossed Lake Pontchartrain to ply their wares, including the Choctaw Indians from St. Tammany Parish, who sold herbs such as filé for gumbo. As varied as the offerings was the mix of languages spoken, a "Tower of Babel" sound filling the air. As late as 1935, New Orleans had 19 public markets, among those the French, Tremé, Claiborne and Poydras Markets.

Many appetizing treats to satisfy a sweet tooth were sold by the praline lady, who cooled her candies with palmetto fans or strips of brown wrapping paper.

STREET VENDORS
Housewives unable or unwilling to travel to city markets were happy to purchase their food and housekeeping supplies from the many popular street vendors known both for their wares and the cries announcing their arrival. And the wares were plentiful – coffee, cakes, pies, pecans, meats, fish, wine, fruits and vegetables, charcoal, rags, flowers, umbrellas, bottles and brooms. The cymbal man sold doughnuts and crullers, favorites with the Creoles. The corn meal man offered fresh corn meal right from the mill. The fruit and candy ladies made their way along city streets, baskets filled with goods propped on their heads, among them the popular cala lady who sold rice fritters from a wooden bowl. Services such as knife grinding and vending, chimney sweeping and stoop scrubbing were offered door to door. And then there was the clothespole man, wearing his derby hat and yelling "clo-o-othespoles," selling the long poles that were sharp on one end and forked on the other, used to raise slack clotheslines to dry laundry.

A 3623 Milk Cart, New Orleans, La.

Dear Ruth: Here's a typical scene. Will write to you as soon as I get time. Lovingly, Maude.

CREOLE MILKMAN *The rumbling cart, the hooves and accompanying bell were as good as any alarm signifying morning. The milkman had arrived with his horse leading the way. It was a great way to start the day. There were no cartons or plastic containers used in this dairy; milk was poured from a large can into your pitcher. A delicious New Orleans delicacy, Creole cream cheese, with a slight buttermilk taste, was also peddled from the milkman's cart.*

WAFFLE MAN *A hot breakfast on the move was sold by Matthew Andrew Antoine Desire Dekemel, better known as "Buglin' Sam the Waffle Man," a professional musician who specialized in playing jazz tunes on his regulation army bugle. The sugar-coated hot waffles were freshly made in his cart during the 1920s and 30s, and he signaled his arrival as often with a blow on his horn as with the sound of a chime.*

◀ The window displays at D.H. Holmes were elaborate, but they became especially magical at Christmas time.

▾ The restaurant in Canal Street's D.H. Holmes fed shoppers and the working crowd as the Don Chase Orchestra played from its bandstand.

THE ORCHESTRA STAND IN HOLMES RESTAURANT. NEW ORLEANS. LA.

D.H. HOLMES

Daniel Henry Holmes established his store in 1842, and in doing so created one of the earliest department stores in the United States. The original location was on Chartres Street, but most locals remember the four-story Gothic structure on Canal Street which was a traditional holiday destination for families. The revered, old clock in front of D.H. Holmes was a popular meeting spot and was made famous in the Pulitzer-Prize winning novel A Confederacy of Dunces *by John Kennedy Toole. The department store was sold in 1989, and is now the Chateau Sonesta Hotel.*

◂ Maison Blanche introduced Mr. Bingle in the 1950s, and over the years the snowman achieved a popular, cult-like status.

MAISON BLANCHE

Founded in the late 1890s, Maison Blanche became another popular department store in downtown New Orleans. Founded by S.J. Schwartz, Maison Blanche was located on the corner of Canal and Dauphine Streets, beginning in the Mercier Building. A new multi-level, white structure housing the store was built in 1907. It closed during World War I to conserve fuel for the war effort, but reopened after the war. The department store featured the first escalators in the city in 1926, and the building housed the studios for WSMB radio. The store occupied the first five floors, with the rest of the building providing office space for numerous professionals, including doctors and dentists. But what most recall about Maison Blanche is a small snowman with holly wings and an ice cream cone hat named "Mr. Bingle," who, with a "jingle, jangle, jingle," announced the start of the Christmas season. Maison Blanche closed in 1998, and was renovated to become the present Ritz-Carlton Hotel.

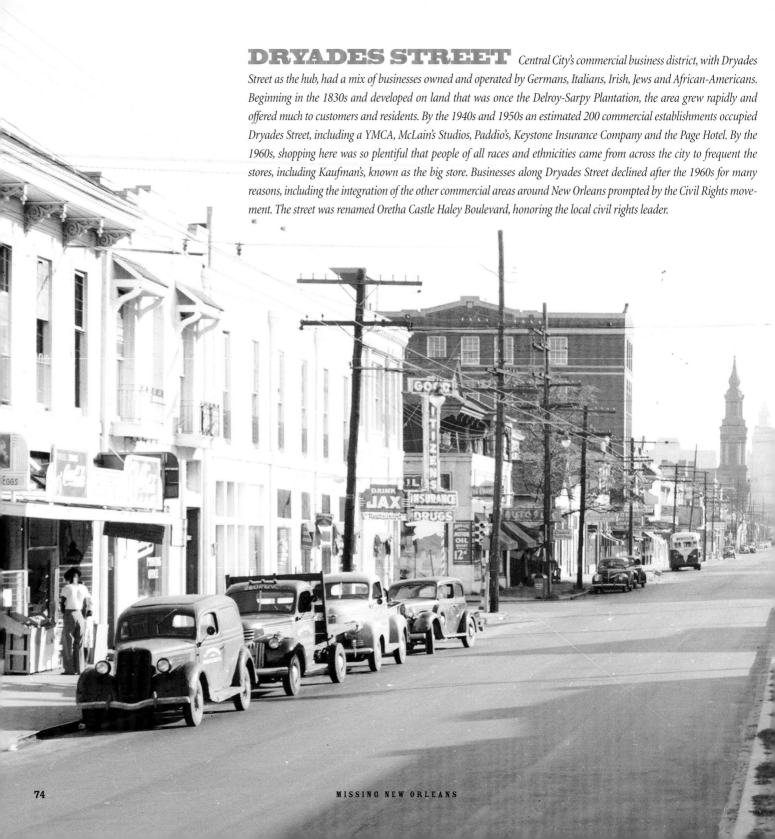

DRYADES STREET *Central City's commercial business district, with Dryades Street as the hub, had a mix of businesses owned and operated by Germans, Italians, Irish, Jews and African-Americans. Beginning in the 1830s and developed on land that was once the Delroy-Sarpy Plantation, the area grew rapidly and offered much to customers and residents. By the 1940s and 1950s an estimated 200 commercial establishments occupied Dryades Street, including a YMCA, McLain's Studios, Paddio's, Keystone Insurance Company and the Page Hotel. By the 1960s, shopping here was so plentiful that people of all races and ethnicities came from across the city to frequent the stores, including Kaufman's, known as the big store. Businesses along Dryades Street declined after the 1960s for many reasons, including the integration of the other commercial areas around New Orleans prompted by the Civil Rights movement. The street was renamed Oretha Castle Haley Boulevard, honoring the local civil rights leader.*

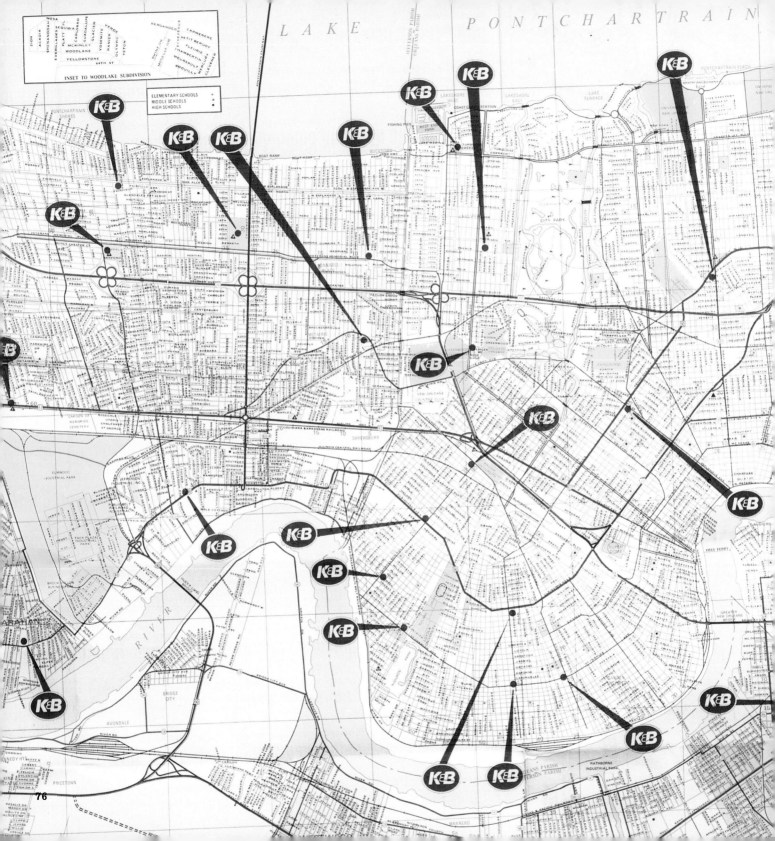

K&B *Gustave Katz and Sydney Besthoff started with one K&B drugstore on Canal Street in 1905 and the chain grew to 186 stores by the 1990s. The trademark big K&B purple signs seemingly covered every corner in New Orleans and served as landmark guides to getting around the city. K&B's slogan was, "Only the Best," and the chain branded its own line of products, including cough drops and ice cream. Its soda fountains were also popular. Rite Aid bought the "purple wonder" in 1997.*

SCHWEGMANN'S *The Schwegmann family proved it was far ahead of the times when it came to "making groceries" in a big way. Established by German immigrant John Garret Schwegmann, Schwegmann stores sold bread and fresh fruit in various locations from 1869-1891 in the Bywater neighborhood where many German immigrants had settled. With the opening of the Piety and Burgundy Street store in 1891, the first permanent Schwegmann's was established. Early stores were full-service operations, with customers handing their lists to employees who would fill orders, but by 1939 the idea of self-service shopping was introduced, to the dismay of some. By 1946 the Schwegmann family opened their first Giant Super Market at the corner of Elysian Fields and St. Claude Avenues. When the Old Gentilly Road location opened in 1957, it was the world's largest, with 155,000 square feet of shopping space, aisles named after French Quarter streets, a barber shop, beauty salon, attorney, notary, and more, employing 400-500 people depending on the season. Eventually the company would include gas stations, pharmacies and branches of the Schwegmann Bank. The grocery corporation came to an end in 1996.*

In addition to promoting itself, the grocery company
used its bags for political endorsements.

Schwegmann

◄ When the new 90,000 square foot Airline store
opened in 1950, it did so with everything but cash
registers. The employees used adding machines
to total up purchases, making change from money
in cigar boxes.

◀ Andrew Higgins' company produced so many vessels during World War II, waterways such as Bayou St. John, near one of his largest plants in City Park, resembled a military warehouse on water.

▼ Higgins' employees, including women and African-Americans who earned equal wages, donned steel hats and identification buttons while advancing the war effort in New Orleans.

HIGGINS BOATS
He was born in Nebraska, but Andrew Jackson Higgins left his mark on New Orleans, where his boat building factories produced numerous military vessels, including what General Dwight D. Eisenhower considered one the most crucial instruments to the Allies' success: LCVP, better known as Higgins Boats. In 1938, Higgins had one factory in New Orleans and employed 75 people. By 1943, Higgins' company had grown to seven factories and employed 20,000 workers, who built 20,000 LCVP, which were imperative during the D-Day invasion of Europe. He tested his military vessels in Bayou St. John and Lake Pontchartrain, as he waged a war against time and production to help the Allies.

Pg. 55 Canal Street (postcard), C. B. Mason, New Orleans, Louisiana; Pg. 56 The French Market – Selling Gumbo (sketch), *Louisiana 100 Years Ago: Vol. II*, compiled by Skip Whitson, Sun Publishing Company, © 1976 by Skip Whitson; Pg. 56 Unloading Bananas from Ship Side, New Orleans, Louisiana, Post Card Specialties, 1935, courtesy of The Historic New Orleans Collection; Pg. 57 Godchaux's medal, photograph by Joe Bergeron, courtesy of Laura Lee Kileen, Fitzgerald Advertising; Pg. 57 K&B phone blotter, courtesy of Sydney Besthoff; Pg. 58 Citizens' Bank Building, courtesy of The Historic New Orleans Collection; Pg. 59 Ten Dollar bill, photograph by Joe Bergeron, courtesy of Bergeron Gallery; Pg. U. S. Mint postcard; Pg. 61 Coins, Photograph by Joe Bergeron, courtesy of Bergeron Gallery; Pg. 62 Cotton Exchange exterior, courtesy of The Historic New Orleans Collection; Pg. 63 Cotton Exchange interior, *Illustrated Newspaper*, Frank Leslie, July 6, 1889; Pg. 64 Andres Molinary, Old Gentilly Road, 1890, gift of the Roger Houston Ogden Collection; Pg. 65 Tremé Market, courtesy of New Orleans Public Library; Pg. 66 Praline Lady, photograph by C. Bennett Moore, courtesy of Bergeron Gallery; Pg. 67 Clothespole Man, courtesy of The Historic New Orleans Collection; Pg. 68 Milk Cart, New Orleans, Louisiana, courtesy of The Historic New Orleans Collection; Pg. 69 Waffle Man, photograph by Frank Gordon, courtesy of Frank Gordon Gallery; Pg. 70 D. H. Holmes exterior, photography by C. F. Weber, courtesy of Bergeron Gallery; Pg. 71 The orchestra stand in D. H. Holmes Restaurant, courtesy of The Historic New Orleans Collection; Pg. 72 Mr. Bingle, Photograph by Joe Bergeron, courtesy of Bergeron Gallery, from the Collection of Karen Chiapetta; Pg. 73 Maison Blanche exterior, Photograph by C. F. Weber, courtesy of Bergeron Gallery; Pg. 74-75 Dryades Street, photograph by C. F. Weber, courtesy of Bergeron Gallery; Pg. 76 K&B locations map, courtesy of Sydney Besthoff; Pg. 77 K&B storefront, courtesy of The Historic New Orleans Collection; Pg. 77 Cough pastilles, photograph by Joe Bergeron, courtesy of Bergeron Gallery; Pg. 78 Schwegmann's Supermarket exterior, photograph by Joe Bergeron, courtesy of Bergeron Gallery; Pg. 79 Schwegmann's Supermarket bag, photograph by Joe Bergeron, courtesy of Bergeron Gallery; Pg. 80 Higgins Boats on Bayou St. John, courtesy of The National D-Day Museum; Pg. 81 Higgins Boats badge, courtesy of The National D-Day Museum Pg. 81 Higgins Boats helmet, courtesy of The National D-Day Museum; Pg. 82 Schwegmann's Beer can, photograph by Joe Bergeron, courtesy of Bergeron Gallery, from the Collection of Dot Bonnot

Asking the public, "What's wrong with low prices?," John G. Schwegmann protested so-called "Fair Trade" laws and became a champion of customers. Among the products the grocery chain branded were alcoholic beverages, including Schwegmann's Premium Lager Beer.

END OF THE LINE

TRANSPORTATION IN NEW ORLEANS

(Previous Page) The Desire streetcar, pictured in 1947 as it ran through the French Quarter, was the city's most famous line, running between Canal Street and Desire Street until the line was discontinued in 1948 and replaced by city busses. The streetcar was gone, but not forgotten, thanks to playwright Tennessee Williams, a resident of the French Quarter and author of the award-winning play *A Streetcar Named Desire.*

▲ The Spanish Fort trains were electric streetcars carrying pleasure-seekers from downtown to the Spanish Fort amusement park on the Lake until 1932.

Transportation into the city developed initially along the Mississippi River through Lake Ponchatrain to Bayou St. John. Completion of the Old Basin Canal connected Bayou St. John to the Basin Street area, outside the French Quarter. Next, the New Basin Canal was built during the 1830s, using Irish laborers, to create shipping and transportation linkage from the lakefront to the American sector. The terminus of the canal was located near Loyola and Julia streets, near today's railroad station. Beginning in the 1930s, this canal was filled in, eventually serving as the foundation for the interstate highway system into the city.

Steamboats played a central role in the evolution of New Orleans. The steamboat era continued from around 1820 to 1870, and New Orleans was its greatest urban center. Steamboats offered ease and luxury in river transportation, as well as new commercial possibilities, along the Mississippi and Ohio River valleys. Noted ships traveling the Mississippi River in these years included the J.W. White, the Sultana, the Belle of Memphis, the Silver Wave, the Natchez and the Robert E. Lee. In the modern era, the President and the Admiral, as well as paddle wheelers like the Delta Queen, the Mississippi Queen and the Belle of Louisville, maintain those earlier traditions, while the Natchez and its calliope continue to fill the French Quarter with sounds from an earlier era.

Railroads were active here during the 1830s, with the Pontchartrain line, running from the River to the Lake, serving as one of the nation's oldest. The New Orleans and Carrollton, also active in the 1830s, ran from New Orleans to Carrollton, and served as the foundation of the St. Charles streetcar line, the oldest continually running line in the nation. After the Civil War, railroads displaced steamboats, marking the end of an era. Railroads opened the city to new types of tourism and new levels of commercial activity. By the early 20th century, the city had five railroad stations, two designed by leading architects: the Illinois Central station (designed by Louis Sullivan); the Southern Railroad station (designed by Daniel Burnham); the Louisville and Nashville station; the Texas, Pacific, Missouri Pacific terminal; and the Louisiana & Arkansas, Kansas City Southern station.

Like the railroads, streetcars played an important role in the evolution of New Orleans, providing reliable public transportation, while advancing the expansion of outlying neighborhoods. Streetcar activity in the city began with the omnibus lines, drawn by horses, before street rail lines drawn by mules became common. Steam cars were used for a time on the St. Charles line, before the introduction of electric streetcars for the World's Industrial and Cotton Centennial Exposition, in 1884-85. By 1900, electric cars were increasingly common. Canal Street was a hub for many lines, and passengers could travel easily from the Mississippi River to lakefront parks or to others areas, including Carrollton. One streetcar became particularly famous as a result of the Tennessee Williams' play, *A Streetcar Named Desire.*

Following the activities of the Wright Brothers and other air pioneers, a passion for flying developed in America. A series of air shows in New Orleans reflected this, even while steamboats plied the waters of the Mississippi and locomotives filled train sheds downtown. In 1910, aviator John B. Moisant was fatally injured in an air accident over City Park; his name was memorialized later at the opening of the city's international airport, now Louis Armstrong Airport. Earlier, in 1934, a grand Art Deco air terminal opened as the Shushan Airport, located on the lakefront. Though the terminal exterior was covered by later additions, the original interiors and architectural details remain, symbolizing an earlier era of air travel as well as the city's ties to Central and South America, reflected in a floor medallion placing New Orleans as the center of North and South America. By the 1940s, the rapidly evolving pace of air transportation and the coming of the jet age led to the opening of the Moisant Airport in the suburbs, replacing Shushan Airport.

The automobile, like the plane, quickly became a symbol of the 20th century and changed the face and the nature of New Orleans. Though there were only a limited number of paved roads around the city as the 19th century ended, during the early 20th century paved highways developed and increasingly linked New Orleans to the state. During these years, new types of architecture—gas stations, motor courts, motels, strip shopping areas and drive-in restaurants—became common in and around New Orleans. New bridges, including the Huey P. Long Bridge, and projects like the Causeway over Lake Pontchartrain, opened the city to the region and the nation in new ways.

Suburban expansion and the movement away from the city advanced during the 1950s and 1960s with the construction of the new interstate highway system. In New Orleans, historic neighborhoods were altered and properties were destroyed along the path of I-10, including the loss of the historic Claiborne Avenue oaks. An extended legal struggle over a proposed interstate path, across the French Quarter and the city's riverfront, was called the second Battle of New Orleans. The appearance of shopping centers and subdivisions, built along these highways in once remote locations, drew people away from the city to surrounding parishes, contributing to the decline of Canal Street, downtown and older urban neighborhoods.

▲ Designed in 1892, the Illinois Central Railway Station was the only train station famed architect Louis Sullivan designed. Young Frank Lloyd Wright was the architect's assistant during this period.

▼ In the 19th century, the wharves of New Orleans were packed with steamboats, which were usually moored close together, providing an endless sightline of tree-like stacks.

BAYOU ST. JOHN LIGHTHOUSE

The Bayou St. John lighthouse, depicted here by Saint-Aulaire in 1821, was one of the first lighthouses built in the Gulf Coast region. The lighthouse was torn down in 1878 to make way for a new entrance to Bayou St. John on Lake Pontchartrain.

Mississippi River Steamboat with Large Load of Cotton Bales, New Orleans, La.

STEAMBOATS

As more Americans settled along the Mississippi River and the Ohio River Valley, rivers gained importance as a way to transport goods and people. Steamboats traveling to and from New Orleans on the Mississippi River in the 1800s and early 1900s were often floating palaces, with chandeliers, carpets and other luxuries for travelers. They were also at the center of commerce. Between 1830 and 1840, New Orleans was growing into one of the greatest ports in America, serving as a gateway between the Mississippi Valley and the rest of the world. From 1859 to 1860, there were approximately 4,000 steamboat arrivals in New Orleans. The hauling of cargo on those boats in and out of the city's port filled the levee along the Mississippi River with non-stop activity.

▸ In its heyday, during post-reconstruction, the city's port bustled with steamboat activity, with smoke pouring from the stacks along the Mississippi River signaling a successful, prosperous industry supporting the New Orleans economy.

L. & N. Station, New Orleans, La.—61

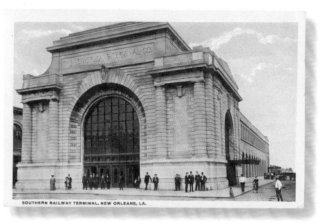

SOUTHERN RAILWAY TERMINAL, NEW ORLEANS, LA.

TRANS-MISSISSIPPI PASSENGER STATION, NEW ORLEANS, LA.

Don't you think this pretty?

UNION STATION PARK, NEW ORLEANS LA

TRAINS *New Orleans had three short-line railroads, the longest one covering 19 miles in the 1830s. After the Civil War, railroads superceded steamboats in popularity for travel, and train travel to and from the city continued to grow, and with it an increase in tourism. By the early 1950s, the flow of passengers and cargo to and from New Orleans was plentiful, thanks in part to the city's five train stations. Among those were the Southern Railway Terminal Station on Canal Street at Basin, the L & N Station on Canal Street, which was used in the opening scene of the movie A Streetcar Named Desire and the Union Station near Loyola Avenue. When the new Union Passenger Terminal opened in 1954, on the site of the previous Illinois Central Station, it signaled the end of the line for the others.*

◄ The Southern Railway Terminal Station on Canal Street at Basin opened in 1908 and was torn down in 1956. It was designed by architect Daniel Burnham, who designed Washington, D.C.'s Union Station.

NEW BASIN CANAL

Commercial competition between the Americans and Creoles extended from within the city to Lake Pontchartrain and led to the American group looking for a way to connect the Faubourg St. Marie, today's Central Business District, to the Lake in the 1830s. The Creoles used Bayou St. John. For the Americans, the answer was the New Basin Canal, a six-mile waterway that ran from Loyola Avenue, near Julia and Howard Streets, along the present-day interstate and Pontchartrain Expressway, to the West End at the Lake. The canal, which cost $1 million, was dug by hand by Irish immigrants from 1832-38. It was a hub for commercial activity, as well as barrel polo races, sculling races and mile-long swimming competitions. The turning basin of the canal was located near today's Union Passenger Terminal. It was filled in segment by segment beginning in 1937. The only stretch of the canal that remains today is where West End Boulevard meets Lakeshore Drive, with the Southern Yacht Club on its west side and the West End lighthouse standing on its eastern bank.

▸ A Celtic cross stands on the neutral ground of West End Boulevard as a monument to the estimated 6,000-10,000 Irish immigrants who died while digging the New Basin Canal.

Additional work on the New Basin Canal after its initial completion in 1838 increased its dimensions to 100-feet in width and 12-feet in depth.

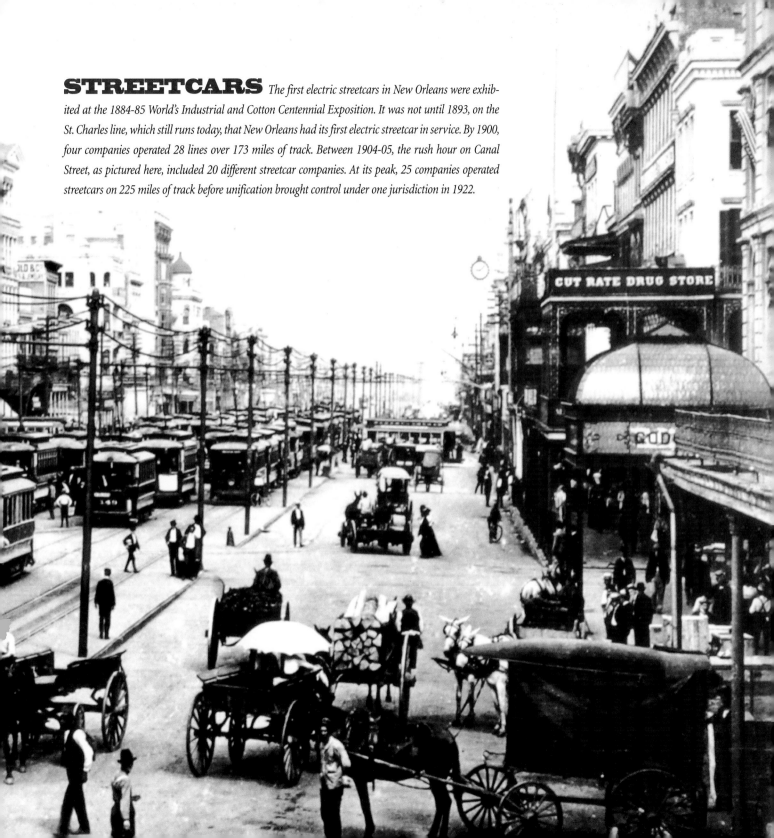

STREETCARS *The first electric streetcars in New Orleans were exhibited at the 1884-85 World's Industrial and Cotton Centennial Exposition. It was not until 1893, on the St. Charles line, which still runs today, that New Orleans had its first electric streetcar in service. By 1900, four companies operated 28 lines over 173 miles of track. Between 1904-05, the rush hour on Canal Street, as pictured here, included 20 different streetcar companies. At its peak, 25 companies operated streetcars on 225 miles of track before unification brought control under one jurisdiction in 1922.*

CUT RATE DRUG STORE

COMMEMORATING THE FORMAL OPENING OF

SHUSHAN AIRPORT

NEW ORLEANS, U.S.A.

SHUSHAN AIRPORT *When it opened in 1934 as the Shushan Airport, named after Levee Board president Abe Shushan, the Lakefront Airport carried a distinctly different look. The airport was built partly on land reclaimed from Lake Pontchartrain, where the Lake meets the Industrial Canal, near the present day University of New Orleans. It was used for flight training during World War II, and today services corporate and private planes.*

While the airport itself is not "missing," what has been lost is the original exterior of the Shushan Airport, which reflected the Art Deco style popular in the 1930s, when the airport was constructed. The building, with its sleek, clean lines, rounded corners and the Shushan named carved into the stone, was eventually covered and remains hidden behind a plain facade.

SHUSHAN
AIRPORT

One of the routes to Lake Pontchartrain from the city was Shell Road, which ran parallel to the New Basin Canal, was built with dirt dug from the canal and had a toll booth next to what is today Metairie Cemetery. In its earliest days, it was a favorite track for men to test the speed of their horses. Before 1910, tolls were collected for use of the road, 6 $\frac{1}{2}$ ¢ for a man on horseback and 24¢ for carriages.

LET THE GOOD TIMES ROLL

AMUSEMENTS FOR NEW ORLEANS

(Previous Page) Swimmers enjoy the waters of Lake Pontchartrain on the shores of Pontchartrain Beach amusement park, located at the end of Elysian Fields Avenue.

▲ The French Opera House was the setting for the Krewe of Comus' Mardi Gras ball on March 7, 1905, as seen on this elaborate invitation.

▲ An admission ticket to the French Opera House for the 1910-1911 season's Sunday matinee allowed this patron seating in the *loge grille*, the latticed stalls.

New Orleans has maintained its reputation as a place for a good time, with Mardi Gras perhaps the most recognized symbol of that reputation. Mardi Gras celebrations have remained an essential part of the city's culture since the antebellum era. Over generations, Mardi Gras krewes have evolved and parade routes have changed, including the removal of Carnival parades from the French Quarter. Mardi Gras maintains its traditions of unique floats and public art forms, created by designers and artists, as well as musical traditions including those heard in the city's many marching and brass bands.

Opera played a critical role in the evolution of the city's cultural life. Beginning in the antebellum era, the French Opera House was a center of Creole culture. Its elegant neo-classical building served as home for opera performances, Carnival balls and as a landmark on Bourbon Street. When it was destroyed by fire in 1919, it marked more than the end of a great public building. It was the end of Creole dominance of the life and culture of the city.

The city's civic leaders, inspired by a series of international fairs, presented the World's Industrial and Cotton Centennial Exposition in 1884-85, marked by a main building that covered 30 acres and Horticulture Hall measuring 600 by 194 feet. The Exposition's electrification and the introduction of electrified street cars to the Exposition site, suggested the progressive vision of Exposition developers and their desire to mark the emergence of the "New South" in New Orleans, as espoused by journalist Henry Grady in Atlanta. The Exposition marked a new era in developing Uptown and the University districts of the city.

Along Lake Pontchartrain, a series of developments marked the city's awareness of the popular Victorian interest in resorts and beachfront activities, offering diverse entertainments for locals and visitors. Increased transportation systems made it easier to travel to the lakefront, where many sought relief from the heat and humidity. Primary attractions there included the West End area, Spanish Fort and Milneburg.

Spanish Fort, located on Bayou St. John, was built upon the ruins of a Spanish Fort from the colonial era. It featured a number of attractions, including a popular amusement park and German beer garden, a series of musical presentations and diverse water sports. Nearby, Pontchartrain Beach offered additional recreational options, expanding over the decades, while during the era of segregation, Lincoln Beach was opened for African-Americans, complete with its own pool and amenities, as well as concert and performance venues.

Uptown, near the site of the 1884-85 Exposition, plans called for the building of a city zoo. Though it was less than a stellar venue, this modest initiative set the foundation for today's Audubon Nature Institute and its diverse components, including the nationally-recognized Audubon Zoo and its downtown

Aquarium of the Americas. And, for those who did not want to travel to the lakefront to swim, a massive new Audubon swimming pool was built, described as one of the nation's largest at that time.

For sports fans, the city was filled with diversions, including yacht racing and other water sports. Baseball was a popular pastime, and New Orleans had its own center at Pelican Stadium. For the football fan, Tulane Stadium served as the home for Tulane football, Sugar Bowls, and several Super Bowls, before the Louisiana Superdome offered a permanent home for these events and the city's professional football team, the New Orleans Saints.

Movie theaters also played a central role in the entertainment life of New Orleans. The major movie palaces were clustered along Canal Street and many additional theaters were scattered in neighborhoods across the city, bringing a sense of community to the collective experience of "going to the movies." After the war, the development of drive-in movie theaters was also notable in less developed parts of the city. Naturally, as viewing habits changed, theaters and drive-ins closed, and new uses were found for these properties.

▲ "Over the Rhine," the restaurant and beer garden with outdoor dining and oompah music, was a popular spot accessible to patrons by a footbridge that crossed Bayou St. John from the Spanish Fort Amusement Park.

▼ Swan boats once carried passengers through Audubon Park on its winding lagoons at a cost of 10¢ per ride.

▶ Opera glasses like these were imported from Paris and sold at the A. B. Griswold Store.

◀ An illustration by British artist Alfred R. Waud, rendered while on assignment in New Orleans for a Boston magazine, depicts ladies and gentlemen in the French Opera House's *corbeille* (dress circle) level.

FRENCH OPERA HOUSE

The French Opera House, built in 1859 on the corner of Bourbon and Toulouse Streets, celebrated the Creoles' love of the opera, with most performances in French. Accommodating over 1,500 people, the Neo-Classical structure hosted many receptions, celebrations and Carnival balls. The stage was framed by Corinthian columns. The latticed stalls, or loges grilles, afforded privacy, especially for pregnant ladies and people in mourning. A rehearsal theater for performers was on the top floor. The French Opera House attracted renowned national and international performers until it burned down in 1919. The site is occupied today by the Ramada Plaza Hotel, The Inn on Bourbon.

▸ The program for the French Opera House's 1919-20 season proclaimed another exciting year of art and festivities. Soon after the season opened, the French Opera House burned down.

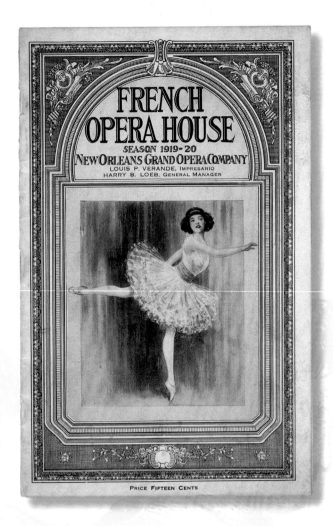

FRENCH
OPERA HOUSE
SEASON 1919-20
NEW ORLEANS GRAND OPERA COMPANY
LOUIS P. VERANDE, IMPRESARIO
HARRY B. LOEB, GENERAL MANAGER

PRICE FIFTEEN CENTS

▸ Designed by the firm of Gallier & Esterbrook, the French Opera House was regularly packed, bottom to top, for performances, as seen in this image of premiere night, circa 1901. The *quatriémes* (fourth tier) was reserved for African-American audiences.

FRENCH QUARTER PARADES

Mardi Gras parade routes through the French Quarter streets were once common, with balconies perfect for parade watching, especially in the 19th and early-20th centuries. With Carnival balls immediately following parades hosted at the French Opera House before its demise, and later at the Municipal Auditorium, a route through the French Quarter proved a sensible destination for many krewes. Growing concern regarding fire coupled with an increase in float size that made navigation of the Quarter's narrow streets and sharp turns more difficult contributed to city officials putting an end to parading in the French Quarter. The last French Quarter parade tied to a Carnival krewe was in 1972.

◀ John McCrady's painting, *The Parade*, depicts the mad revelry of Mardi Gras passing his French Quarter studio. *(Ogden Museum Permanent Collection)*

▶ Glass beads made in Europe, like these, were once the throw *de riguer* from a passing Mardi Gras float.

▸ Spanning 600 feet in length, Horticulture Hall was the largest conservatory in the world at that time.

HORTICULTURE HALL
The lone building remaining from the 1884-85 World's Industrial and Cotton Centennial Exposition, held in New Orleans, was Horticulture Hall. The large, glass structure housed more than 20,000 fruits and flowers, included a 90-foot tower and an electronically-lit fountain. Following the Exposition, the Hall became the principal attraction in developing Audubon Park. The structure remained a greenhouse, where it housed a collection of exotic plants, and included cages for monkeys and birds, presaging the current Audubon Zoo. The hall was destroyed by a tropical storm in 1915.

The New Basin Canal led to West End on Lake Pontchartrain. The modes of transportation to West End included carriages, steam and electrified trains and automobiles traveling Shell Road.

West End Park and Lake Pontchartrain, New Orleans, La., on the
Illinois Central System.

WEST END The embankment that jutted out 800 feet into Lake Pontchartrain proved the starting point for New Lake End in 1871, when transportation to the area was established by the New Orleans & Lake Railroad transporting passengers to the area. In 1880, the area was renamed West End and by 1890 the West End Hotel was constructed and was a favorite spot for weekend relaxation. Patrons enjoyed restaurants, amusement rides and musical performances staged on a pavilion. A scenic railway built over the water featured the "tunnel of love." The first movies shown outdoors in New Orleans, in 1896, were projected on a large canvas screen in front of the West End bandstand. The area experienced its heyday from the 1880s to the 1920s.

lub 1910

SOUTHERN YACHT CLUB

The Southern Yacht Club, a private club and the second oldest in the United States, was originally founded in 1849 in Pass Christian, Mississippi and included members from New Orleans. In 1879, with 402 members on its roll, the Southern Yacht Club relocated to New Orleans under the leadership of Commodore Emile J. O'Brien, a cotton broker, who spearheaded the construction of a clubhouse built at West End at the cost of $3,355. Because the New Basin Canal was a popular waterway for transporting logs and other activities, the clubhouse's pilings were damaged over time, necessitating the construction of a new structure, which opened in 1900, costing $8,314. Over the years, it underwent a series of renovations and additions, and stood until 1948, when it was razed for a modern structure made of steel and reinforced concrete. In 1949, the new clubhouse was dedicated, the same year the Municipal Yacht Harbor was opened, and the public New Orleans Yacht Club was chartered by the State.

◄ People often socialized on the walkway that led to the Southern Yacht Club's second clubhouse at the turn of the century. The structure went through a series of renovations until 1948.

SPANISH FORT

Built as a colonial fort by the French in 1701, Spanish Fort was a acquired by the Spanish and rebuilt in 1779. The land was sold in 1823, and by 1828 the area included a bathhouse and the elegant Pontchartrain Hotel, which featured a pleasure garden. It remained a popular resort area, reaching its peak by 1883, when Spanish Fort had grown to include a casino, a theater where concerts were presented and where author Oscar Wilde was said to have lectured. Across the Bayou was the popular German beer garden "Over the Rhine." In 1911, an amusement park was added, the predecessor to the first Pontchartrain Beach, featuring the roller coaster, The Wildcat. Spanish Fort's popularity waned as the rest of the area along the Lake's shore improved.

remnants of the fort remain on the levee bordering the Bayou.

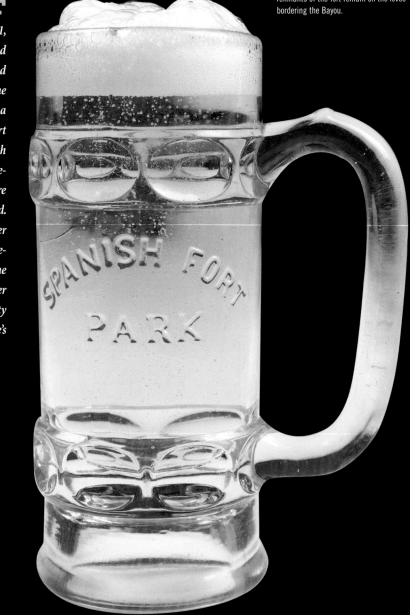

Originally built to protect the city, Spanish Fort became a source for amusement and included such attractions as a concert hall and alligator pond.

CONCERT HALL & GARDEN, SPANISH FORT

ALLIGATOR POND, SPANISH FORT

The Spanish Fort Amusement Park reached its peak in the early 1900s and was proclaimed the "Coney Island of the South."

PONTCHARTRAIN BEACH I

Built on filled land reclaimed from Lake Pontchartrain by the Orleans Levee Board across from Spanish Fort, the first Pontchartrain Beach amusement park opened in 1928, and was replete with an arcade, concessions, rides, bathhouses and a boardwalk. One of the attractions was a roller coaster called the Big Dipper. The amusement park endured through the Depression and remained open until 1938, when it was moved to a new location further east along the Lake's shore. One of its popular rides, The Bug, made the move, surviving until the amusement park's last days in its new location.

Pontchartrain Beach in the 1920s and early 1930s, when it was located across from Spanish Fort, was a popular bathing spot.

Owner Harry Batt, Sr. supervised the relocation of Pontchartrain Beach eastward in 1938 to its new site at the end of Elysian Fields Avenue, in an area known as Milneburg. All that remains today is the Milneburg Lighthouse.

▾ Where Pontchartrain Beach visitors once loved "the thrilling rides and laughed 'til they split their sides," the University of New Orleans' Research & Technology Park now stands.

PONTCHARTRAIN BEACH II *In 1939, Pontchartrain*

Beach opened as a new amusement park. Its location was soon surrounded by military installations, fostering the park's popularity in the 1940s. Rides eventually included the Wild Mouse, the Smokey Mary and a ferris wheel that offered a grand view of Lake Pontchartrain. A looming clown's head marked the entrance to the Cockeyed Circus, with tilted floors and funny mirrors. Entertainment varied, from an arcade, miniature golf, dolphin shows, fireworks, beauty contests and diving demonstrations to rock-n-rollers like the Everly Brothers and Elvis, who performed on the park's stage. The symbol of the park was the Zephyr roller coaster; while it was loud, fast and unforgettable, almost as memorable were its long waiting lines. Pontchartrain Beach closed in 1983.

LINCOLN BEACH *In 1939, a quarter mile stretch of beach in New Orleans East in an area called Little Woods was set aside by the Orleans Levee Board as a swimming area for African-Americans. By the early 1950s, in the era of segregation, Lincoln Beach had become a popular destination with amusement park rides, games, restaurants, a swimming pool and diving shows. Musical acts including Fats Domino and the Ink Spots performed on its stage. Lincoln Beach remained prominent in the lives of New Orleans' African-American citizens until 1964, when segregation ended. The only thing that remains is the rusted sign marking Lincoln Beach's entrance.*

Divers line up to take the plunge in Lincoln Beach's popular swimming pool in the summer of 1959.

ORIGINAL AUDUBON ZOO

While Audubon Park housed monkeys and birds in Horticulture Hall, the central idea for a zoo began to take shape in 1919 when Daniel D. Moore, then president of the Audubon Park Auxiliary Association, put up $500 as seed money. In 1924, the zoo welcomed its first animals. National attention was focused on the zoo in the 1950s with the hatching of the first whooping cranes in captivity. Attention was also focused on the zoo for the less than stellar housing conditions it afforded the animals. From its humble beginnings the zoo, which operates under the auspices of the Audubon Nature Institute, has evolved into its consistent ranking as one of the top ten zoos in the country.

SWIMMING POOL, AUDUBON PARK, NEW ORLEANS, LA.—153

AUDUBON POOL *Johnny Weissmuller, an Olympic champion swimmer and "Tarzan" in the movies, was on hand for the opening ceremonies of the Audubon Park Pool in 1928. More than 160 yards long and 50 yards wide, the pool, when it opened, was the largest in the South and second largest in the nation, with slides and a huge fountain in the middle. It closed in 1962 when it did not comply with a ruling to integrate. In 1970 the New Orleans Recreation Department took over operations, and the Audubon Pool re-opened. It was renamed after Civil Rights leader Whitney Young. The pool closed in 1994, and today is the site of a parking lot and soccer fields.*

The Audubon Pool, located uptown near Magazine Street where the entrance to the current Zoo is located, could accommodate more than 2,000 people.

PELICAN STADIUM

Built on land once occupied by White City Amusement Park at Tulane and Carrollton Avenues, Pelican Stadium was originally called Heinemann Park from 1915-38 for manager Alexander Julius Heinemann. Renamed Pelican Stadium, the park spanned 458 feet by 610 feet, one of the largest in the country at that time. Pelican Stadium provided a grass and dirt stage for popular Major League players, including Shoeless Joe Jackson, who played with the team during the 1910 season, leading them to their second Southern Association pennant, prior to the stadium's construction. Other legendary Pelicans included Mel Ott, "Oyster Joe" Martina, Cotton Knaupp, Dixie Walker and manager Larry Gilbert. Another team manager, Abner Powell, considered "the father of the Pelicans," introduced the "rain check" and the idea of covering the field with tarpaulins, and brought "ladies day" to New Orleans fans. Pelican Stadium's mid-city location next to a rail line offered easy access for residents from across the city. It remained home to the Pelicans for 43 years, as well as local African-American teams including the Black Pelicans. The Pelicans played in the stadium through the 1957 season, and the park was torn down, making way for the Fountainbleau Motor Hotel. The team played in present day Tad Gormley Stadium for another two seasons before disbanding.

FRITZ, NEW ORLEANS

THE SUGAR BOWL
(TULANE STADIUM)
NEW ORLEANS, LA

TULANE STADIUM

At one time, it was the largest steel-structure stadium in the nation. Tulane Stadium, built on land that was once a sugar plantation, was constructed in 1926 and fronted Willow Street on the campus of Tulane University. It started small, and with expansion grew to hold 80,985 people. The stadium played host to many Sugar Bowl games and three Super Bowls. When Tulane fans and later professional football's New Orleans Saints' fans packed the place and pounded on the steel, the noise could be heard for blocks. The Green Wave and the Saints eventually moved play to the Louisiana Superdome in 1975, leaving the old structure open for high school games before being torn down in 1980, making room for student housing and a recreational facility.

COLORAMIC RAINBOW BALLROOM

ALL-STEEL EXCURSION STEAMER PRESIDENT ON THE MISSISSIPPI

THE PRESIDENT

The riverboat President, billed "the wondership of the Mississippi," regaled New Orleans and the Mississippi River with cruises and performers such as Louis Armstrong, Alvin Alcorn and Danny Barker. Originally built in 1924 as the Cincinnati, she was refurbished in 1932 under new ownership for entertainment excursions and renamed the President. In 1941, the President's home port became New Orleans, where she was a popular floating music venue for locals, with such headliners as Dizzy Gillespie, Lionel Hampton, Doctor John, B.B. King and Professor Longhair. The President remained in New Orleans until 1985, when she was sold and returned to St. Louis. In 1989, the President was designated a National Historic Landmark. Today, she is a docked casino moored in Mississippi.

◄ Prior to World War II, the President, a five-deck luxury steamboat, carried passengers and entertainers, as far north as Minnesota and as far south as New Orleans year round.

On the grounds of Pontchartrain Beach, the popular Bali Hái at the Beach restaurant, with its entrance marked by this sign, conjured up balmy tropical nights with a Polynesian atmosphere and an Asian-inspired menu. Popular specialty cocktails included the Tiki Bowl, Navy Grog, Bora-Bora and the Fogg Cutter, "the uncrowned king of the exotic drinks."

DOWN THE LINE
VICES IN NEW ORLEANS

(Previous Page) E.J. Bellocq's photograph *Girls Playing Cards* (c. 1911-13) depicts the ladies of Storyville during their leisure hours.

▲ A matchbook promotes O'Dwyer Brothers, a popular gambling hall.

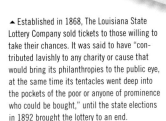

▲ Established in 1868, The Louisiana State Lottery Company sold tickets to those willing to take their chances. It was said to have "contributed lavishly to any charity or cause that would bring its philanthropies to the public eye, at the same time its tentacles went deep into the pockets of the poor or anyone of prominence who could be bought," until the state elections in 1892 brought the lottery to an end.

In addition to its more high-minded entertainments, New Orleans has never been reluctant to offer a fuller range of entertainment options to its residents and visitors. From its beginnings, when flatboats and keelboats unloaded along the riverfront and crews went searching for a good time, New Orleans happily responded to demands—including drinking, gambling, prostitution and other forms of entertainment. The city nurtured diverse forms of fighting, ranging from cockfighting and dog fighting, to serving as a critical location for the evolution of American boxing history. For others, dueling served as a way to resolve issues of "honor," and contributed to the need for new cemetery facilities across the city.

The River brought people many downriver, searching for entertainment on a variety of levels in the city. Initially these diversions were found near the wharf areas, in locations like Gallatin Street, and the area called "The Swamp." By 1897, thanks to the efforts of Alderman Sidney Story, who wanted to control prostitution by confining it to a limited district, the New Orleans City Council approved the formation of the area called Storyville. Storyville only existed for a period of 20 years, from 1897 until 1917, when the Navy banned it.

During the time of its existence, Storyville became widely known for many reasons. The larger district contained approximately 250 houses, with over 2,000 working women, including the surrounding lesser houses and neighboring cribs. Tom Anderson was the prominent figure of the district, and women like Lulu White and Josie Arlington were two of the better known madams. All three were high profile members of the larger community. Storyville became known as home to a wide range of amusements, ranging from prostitution to the development of jazz musical venues, where musical "professors" entertained the guests of the diverse houses. E.J. Bellocq created a series of well-known photographs of the women who worked in the district. For the visitor, there was even a descriptive published guide to the district, known as the *Blue Book*.

Horse racing developed as a major sport in the South, and New Orleans became one of the South's major racing centers, reflected in the number of tracks and the active support for the sport in the city. One of the city's first tracks was located along St. Charles Avenue, on the grounds of Live Oak Plantation, beginning in 1820. The Jackson Course opened in 1825, and another, the Eclipse Track developed on the current Audubon Park property in 1837. The Metairie Club developed in 1838, was restructured as the Metairie Jockey Club in 1853, closed during the Civil War, then reopened for a time before it was acquired and converted into a cemetery, today's Metairie Lakelawn cemetery. Racing also took place on the grounds of City Park and is associated today with the prominent Fair Grounds Race Course.

New Orleans was also recognized as one of the nation's leading venues for boxing during the 1880s and 1890s, when the city was filled with gyms and diverse boxing clubs. One of the greatest boxing matches of the 19th century took place in New Orleans in 1892, when John L. Sullivan, who had been heavyweight champion from 1882 to 1892, defended his title against "Gentleman" Jim Corbett. Sullivan lost this fight against Corbett, which took place at the Olympic Boxing Club.

Gambling flourished as well in the city, dating back to well before the antebellum period. When laws in the city seemed to limit or restrict the possibilities, new venues for gambling began to appear outside the Orleans Parish line. New clubs and new establishments opened, including the Club Forest, the Southport and the Beverly, located in Jefferson Parish, and similar clubs in St. Bernard Parish. Politicians and reformers began to call for change, and launched public campaigns against gambling, staging high profile raids and destroying slot machines and gaming tables before the glare of press photographers, and later, before television cameras. In 1951, Senator Estes Kefauver traveled to New Orleans to investigate the city's reputation as a gambling center, and even broadcast his hearings on television.

During the 19th century, New Orleans had served as home to one of the most organized forms of gambling in the nation's history, the Louisiana State Lottery. Nicknamed "The Octopus," it was formed by Charles T. Howard and John A. Morris. The Louisiana State Lottery Company obtained an exclusive operating permit for 25 years, beginning in 1868, based upon a fixed annual donation to Charity Hospital. The lottery became increasingly successful when it enlisted the assistance of two respected figures, General P. G. T. Beauregard and General Jubal A. Early, who supervised the drawings, in a plan devised by Maximilian Dauphin. Before long, there were Louisiana Lottery ticket agents working in cities across the nation, including New York, Boston and Chicago, and massive amounts of money flowed back, often through the mails, to lottery organizers. The passage of a state law prohibiting all lotteries in Louisiana after 1895 finally put an end to "The Octopus."

▶ A vixen adorns an invitation promoting "The Ball of the Two Well Known Gentlemen," a notorious Mardi Gras celebration at Odd Fellows Hall, where the belles and maskers were prostitutes, madams and pimps.

DUELING

Alcohol, money and gambling flowed freely and ill tempers in New Orleans were not far behind. Someone's life could be at risk if someone else felt slighted or cheated, and dueling was considered the accepted way of settling a dispute. As the fear of losing one's honor was said to be greater than the dread of dying, restoring one's honor led to the proliferation of fencing masters around town, as well as a young man's necessity to become proficient in the use of firearms. Popular places to defend one's honor included City Park or the Halfway House.

▸ The weapons in duels could be as barbaric as shards of glass, as elegant as swords or simple and quick as pistols, like this French dueling pistol with an octagonal barrel and walnut finish that fired 50 caliber metal balls.

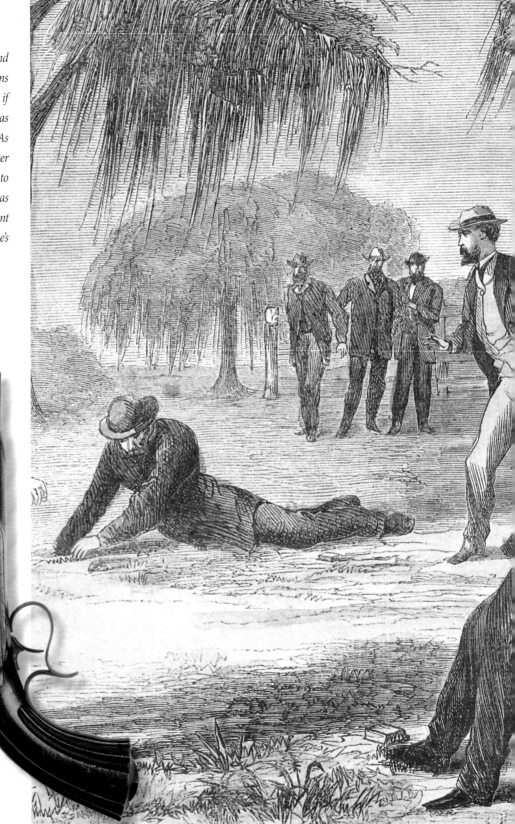

For a brief interval, Exchange Passage, later known as Exchange Alley, was New Orleans' most important street of commerce, serving as a four-block thruway to the St. Louis Hotel from Canal Street. Among the businesses along the alley were shops, saloons, coffee houses, restaurants, and fencing studios, where one could master the sport. The last block of Exchange Alley, between Conti and St. Louis Streets, was torn down in 1905 to build what is today the Louisiana Supreme Court on Royal Street.

◄ Alfred Waud attended a duel in City Park in 1866 between the husband of an opera singer and another member of the cast who had given him "cause for jealousy," as depicted in this illustration by Waud.

THE SWAMP *In the early 1800s, patrons of the part of town located ten blocks from the Mississippi River in the Girod Street area known as the "Swamp," had to be gritty and cautious. Frequented mostly by rough flatboatmen who moored their boats nearby, the Swamp was reputed to be the toughest part of town. The one-story neighborhood was home to dancehalls, gambling dens, flop-houses, excess and violence. Refuge could be found at places like the House of Rest for Weary Boatmen and the Sure Enuf Hotel, which was presided over by rotund Mother Colby and later Frederick Krause, also known as "Crazy Bill." The prostitutes knew how to ply their wares and weapons, if needed. For those with mettle, there were bordellos and simple saloons. For a cheap price, food, lodging and a lady were available for the night. It was said that no city policeman in his right mind would venture within shotgun range of the Swamp in its heyday.*

GALLATIN STREET
It was a short turnpike for riffraff that, rumor has it, became known at one time as "the most dangerous place on earth." Gallatin Street in 1840-70s was a two-block long alley from the French Market to the Mint filled with saloons, gin mills, dance houses, thieves, prostitutes and drug traffic. The area was considered a safehouse for tough characters like Mike Haden, strong-armed madam, America Williams and Joe the Whipper. Gallatin Street was no place for the meek and was known as a "port of missing men." It could be so brutal that police ventured there only in groups. The river side of the street was torn down by the WPA in the 1930s, and today the area is home to the flea market in the French Quarter.

BOXING *Following the Civil War, New Orleans was a mecca for boxing, bare-knuckled style, though the sport was illegal in Louisiana until 1890. Described as "the ring capital of the world" during the 1880s and 90s, most boxers of note appeared in New Orleans. Louisiana was the first state to legalize gloved boxing in 1890, and places like the Olympic Club on Royal Street flourished, hosting big-name fights. The Olympic Club was the site of the longest fight in ring history. When Andy Bowen and Jack Burke battled 110 rounds, seven hours, 19 minutes to a draw. Another notable fight featured a heavyweight world championship clash between John L. Sullivan and "Gentleman" Jim Corbett in 1892. Corbett won and earned $25,000.*

JOHN L. SULLIVAN AND JAS. J. CORBETT
GRAND GLOVE CONTEST FOR THE
HEAVYWEIGHT CHAMPIONSHIP OF THE WORLD
AT THE OLYMPIC CLUB.
PURSE $25,000.
WEDNESDAY, SEPTEMBER 7th 1892.
NINE O'CLOCK P.M.
ENTRANCE CHARTRES ST.
TICKETS $15.00

◀ Achille Peretti rendered this *Portrait of John L. Sullivan* in 1892. The fighter, known as "The Boston Strong Boy," was the heavyweight champion of the world from 1882 to 1892. *(Ogden Museum Permanent Collection)*

▲ The leading athletic club in New Orleans in the 1890s was the Olympic Club, which included a bar, library, billiard room, dining room and lounging rooms. It also played host to numerous high-stakes prizefights, and spectators were willing to pay the high price of admission.

STORYVILLE

In the late 1880s, prostitution in New Orleans, in particular in the French Quarter and north of Canal Street, was ever-expanding and with little regulation. In 1897, the City Council, looking to gain some semblance of control over these activities, supported an ordinance by Alderman Sidney Story, a broker, to confine the trade to one area. By 1898, the legalized "tenderloin district," which people dubbed Storyville, gave the demimondaines almost free rein in a dozen square-block area that is now the Iberville Housing Project. Notorious madams who dominated Storyville included Lulu White, Josie Arlington and Countess Willie V. Piazza. Storyville's doors were open for business until 1917, when operations ceased by order of the United States Navy, in an effort to curb vice in the proximity of armed-services personnel.

Elegant buildings in Storyville housed the brothels, especially the 14 structures in a two-block area known as "Up The Line," where Lulu White's Mahogany Hall was located. A railroad passenger stop on one corner of Basin Street offered easy access for those interested in conducting business in the area.

HILMA BURT'S "MIRROR BALL ROOM" Storyville, N.O.La. 209 No.Basin St. 1902-1903

▲ Famed piano player Jelly Roll Morton plays
among the ladies at Hilma Burt's Mirror Ballroom
on Basin Street, proving the entertainment was
more than just the women in Storyville.

◄ With the emergence of Storyville came the *Blue Book*, a directory to the prostitutes in the district first issued in 1902. The books were bound in blue paper and available for a quarter in bars, hotels, train stations and steamboat landings. The ladies were described by race, physical features and specialties. The book came with this explicit instruction: It was not to be mailed.

City Park Race Track, New Orleans, La.

CITY PARK RACE TRACK *In the area of present-day Tad Gormley Stadium and Roosevelt Mall, the City Park Race Track, with its plush, large grandstand, opened in 1905 on land that had been a dairy farm. The New Orleans Jockey Club operated the track, which attracted large crowds until a crackdown on organized betting at racetracks in 1908. In the track's post-racing days, it was the site for other public events, especially popular aviation shows.*

◄ The spacious grandstand at City Park Race Track remained in its place until 1918, when following a fire at the Fair Grounds Race Course, it was disassembled and moved to that site, and rebuilt. It remained until 1993, lasting until it was destroyed by fire.

Gambling was accompanied by luxury, as seen in this room at the Old Southport Club in Jefferson Parish.

GAMBLING

In 1827, Jack Davis opened the Theatre d'Orleans, which was one of the first real casinos in the United States. By 1850, there were more than 500 gambling houses in New Orleans. Many bars and coffeehouses also had rooms specifically for gambling. Popularity and, initially, legalization of gambling so it could be taxed, helped promote the spread of gaming establishments from Orleans to Jefferson and St. Bernard Parishes. The gamesmanship was as colorful and varied as the chips and slot machines until U.S. Senator Estes Kefauver brought his national crusade to shut down organized crime and gambling to Louisiana in the early 1950s.

Seymour Fogel's *New Orleans Ladies* presents an artistic rendering of "cribs," the decaying hovels occupied by prostitutes plying their trade, the furnishings consisting of a bed, a table and a chair. This distinctive New Orleans architectural form remains in structures still standing in parts of the French Quarter, evidenced by rows of doors and shutters situated close to each other along a city block, in close proximity to what was once Storyville. *(Ogden Museum Permanent Collection)*

RAMPART STREET BLUES

THE WRECKING BALL IN NEW ORLEANS

(Previous Page) The "Three Sisters," designed by James Gallier Sr. and James H. Dakin, were three identical two-story Greek Revival residential structures built in 1834. Located on North Rampart Street between Bienville and Iberville Streets in the French Quarter, the buildings were demolished by the 1960s to the dismay of many, and today is the site of an automobile service center and parking lot.

▲ Following an outbreak of yellow fever and other deadly diseases, the Hebrew Benevolent Association opened the first Widows and Orphans Home in 1856 on Jackson Avenue and Chippewa Street, for women and children left bereft by the death of husbands and fathers. A second home, seen here, was built in 1881 at present-day St. Charles and Jefferson Avenues. The second building became the Jewish Community Center (JCC) by the late 1940s and was torn down in 1963, when a new JCC was erected on the property.

During every stage of the city's evolution, earlier structures and institutions made way for the new, reflecting the inevitable "march of progress," and leaving a toll of loss across the Crescent City. Much of the city's earliest architecture was lost in the fires of 1788 and 1794, removing many French influences and allowing the Spanish influence to mark the older quarter of the city in distinctive ways. One of the most dramatic areas of loss during the 20th century was the Rampart Street area with its many stores, hotels, clubs and related musical traditions.

After the ongoing loss of historic structures in the French Quarter, including the iconic St. Louis Hotel and the French Opera House, and the demolition of a wide range of nearby properties to make way for a new, and recently restored, Louisiana Supreme Court building, the Vieux Carré Commission was formed to protect the architectural and historical character of the district. Similar organizations were formed in Charleston, South Carolina, and in Natchez, Mississippi, to protect the historic districts of those Southern cities as well.

One of the areas of town that has been significantly altered over the years is Lee Circle, originally called Tivoli Circle, before the dedication of the Robert E. Lee Monument in 1884. Structures now missing there include the New Orleans Public Library (1908), financed by Andrew Carnegie, and built upon the foundations of the old Carrollton Railroad Depot; a Moorish-designed gas station and garage, built in 1926; the nearby Temple Sinai, built in 1872, the first home for the city's oldest Reform Jewish congregation; and a German singing hall, the Saengerbund, built in 1890 for a singing festival in New Orleans. Little of the original architecture of the circle remains today, with the exception of the residence now functioning as the Circle Bar, the Lee Monument and the Howard Memorial Library (1889), now known as the Patrick F. Taylor Library, at The Ogden Museum of Southern Art.

Neighborhoods changed and were dramatically altered, as was the case in the Tremé area, when construction of the I-10 elevated expressway moved through the Claiborne Avenue area, destroying the historic oak trees that had served as proud symbols in this public space for generations. Still a gathering point for neighborhood citizens, and a marching site for Mardi Gras Indians under the elevated highway, the memory of these trees lingers, as commemorated in a series of painted oaks adorning the interstate's concrete support.

New Orleans developed an extensive medical history and medical community over the years, with an impressive list of hospital and medical teaching institutions located in the city's medical district. Two important medical centers that have been lost are Hotel Dieu and Sara Mayo. Hotel Dieu was the oldest privately operating hospital, in terms of continuous operation, in the city, operated by the Daughters of Charity. Sara Mayo operated as a noted and highly respected training facility for African-American doctors.

A related change in the city, after 1905, was the disappearance of the countless number of cisterns in the city. Though seldom architectural monuments, they were symbols of the storage of residential and commercial water prior to the creation of a public water and sewage system. Additionally, they were treatment sites for mosquito infestations and the last cases of Yellow Fever in the city.

Well into the middle of the 20th century, the city served as the home of five railroad stations. The opening of a new terminal on Loyola Avenue, and the desire of city fathers to bring a more "modern" look to the city, led to the eventual loss of all five of these structures, including one designed by Louis Sullivan and one designed by Daniel Burnham. Another transportation related loss was the removal of the Canal Street streetcar line in 1964, and its replacement by a series of new buses. However, unlike many of the other losses, this one proved to be reversible, as evident in the rebuilding and reopening of the Canal Street line in 2004.

For members of the city's architecture and design community, the loss of the Rivergate Convention Center on Canal Street was a stunning development. The Rivergate facility, recognized for its engineering systems and creative use of concrete in its design, was erected in 1968. After less than 30 years of use, it was demolished in 1995 for the construction of the new Harrah's Casino complex.

▲ With a high-rising cupola on the corner of Canal and Baronne Streets, it was easy to spot the Chess, Checkers and Whist Club, a gentleman's club. It was built in the 1880s, its purpose to "promote the knowledge and encourage the development of the scientific games of Chess, Checkers and Whist." In 1938, it became a drugstore.

▼ Residents and business owners of 19th century New Orleans, unable to use wells to collect rainwater which was preferable to river water, built cisterns. They were, generally neither sanitary or beautiful, although some were decorated with ironwork in an attempt to make them more aesthetically pleasing. They were, however, a breeding ground for mosquitoes and associated deadly diseases such as yellow fever. Landmarks for almost 100 years, they were outlawed in 1918 for health reasons.

▲ Belknaps Fountain was a downtown landmark on Canal Street at Camp Street from early 1870s, where it marked the end of the New Orleans Traction Company's line. The iron fountain, Victorian in style, was richly adorned with miniature steamboats, swans, ducks and cupids powered by water. It stood in its place until 1896, when the traction company donated it to City Park. What happened to the fountain in later years is a mystery.

OLDEST BUILDING IN NEW ORLEANS, LA.

OLDEST BUILDING

The old Spanish-style building on the corner of Ursuline and Chartres Streets, believed by some to have been the oldest building in the Vieux Carré, provided a turning point when it was demolished in 1933, when an automobile service station was built on the site. The reaction to the razing of the building served as a catalyst to the creation of the Vieux Carré Commission to help protect historic buildings.

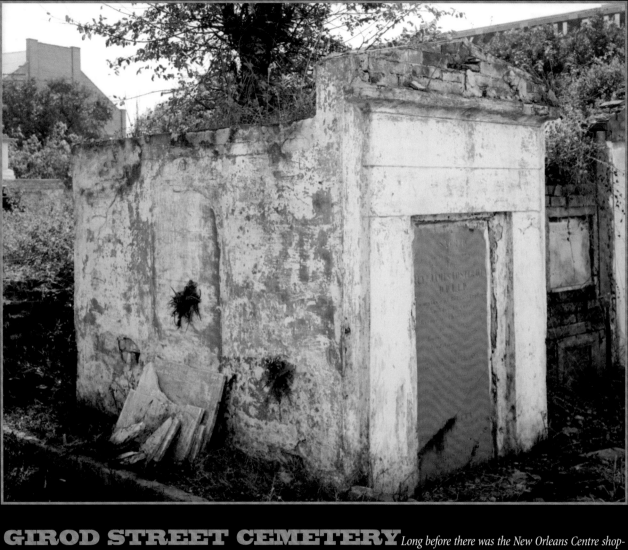

GIROD STREET CEMETERY
Long before there was the New Orleans Centre shopping mall and office tower near the Louisiana Superdome, there was the Girod Street Cemetery. The mall sits atop this former Protestant burial ground, which served as the resting place for many victims of yellow fever and cholera in the 19th century. Thought to be haunted by many, the 135-year old cemetery was deconsecrated in 1957, and the bodies were removed.

RIVERGATE

When it was built in 1968, the Rivergate Convention Center was considered an engineering marvel. The Rivergate was built by the Board of Commissioners of the Port of New Orleans, and spanned six city blocks, bordered by Canal Street and Poydras Street, a growing business artery in the Central Business District. Designed by Nathaniel Curtis Jr. and Arthur Q. Davis, it featured a free-flowing sculptural roof structure that required relatively few support columns, allowing for 132,500 square feet of nearly unobstructed convention space, two levels of underground parking, and accommodating 16,000 people. A proposed expressway slated to sweep across the French Quarter included plans for a tunnel under the Rivergate. The tunnel was built, the city paying $1 million in construction costs, but as the Riverfront expressway was cancelled, it was never used. The Rivergate was demolished in the early 1990s, as depicted in Errol Barron's 1994 painting Demolition of the Rivergate (right) making way for Harrah's Casino.

CLAIBORNE OAKS *The quadruple rows of oak trees along the neutral ground of North Claiborne Avenue provided shade on a hot day, and a great meeting and socializing place for the residents of the Tremé area. The trees were taken down in the mid-1960s for the construction of Interstate-10, when Claiborne Avenue became the alternative site for the proposed French Quarter and Riverfront Expressway. Through the collaborative project, Restore the Oaks, spearheaded by the City of New Orleans Mayor's Division of Housing and Neighborhood Development and the New Orleans African-American Museum, murals were painted on a series of concrete pillars supporting I-10 along North Claiborne Avenue, many memorializing the oaks that once lined the avenue.*

When it was constructed on Lee Circle in 1926, a building as serviceable as this Texaco gas station and garage was designed to conform in style and function to the prestige of the thoroughfare.

LEE CIRCLE *The circular area designed by Barthelemy Lafon in 1807, where St. Charles Avenue meets Howard Avenue, was originally called Place du Tivoli, and was intended to serve as a pleasure garden, with outdoor tables, lamps, shell walkways, a dance floor, and brass bands entertaining those gathered. In the 1840s, Italianate houses just coming into fashion began to populate the Circle. It was renamed Lee Circle after the dedication of the Robert E. Lee monument in 1884. In addition to grand homes, a number of landmark buildings once surrounded the Circle, including the combination Byzantine-Romanesque Temple Sinai, designed by Charles Lewis Hillger in 1872, the Beaux Arts main branch of the New Orleans Public Library replete with a copper dome, designed by Diboll, Owen and Goldstein in 1908, and the Shriners Temple. Today, little is left of what once stood on Lee Circle, one exception being the Howard Memorial Library. It is the only building designed by noted American architect H. H. Richardson built in the South, and was completed after his death in 1889. The library, now called the Patrick F. Taylor Library, is part of The Ogden Museum of Southern Art, University of New Orleans.*

ST. CHARLES AVENUE, SHOWING PUBLIC LIBRARY AND LEE'S MONUMENT, NEW ORLEANS, LA.

LEE CIRCLE, SHOWING LIBRARY AND SHRINERS TEMPLE, NEW ORLEANS, LA.

Pg. 157 Three Sisters, courtesy of New Orleans Public Library; Pg. 158 Jewish Widows and Orphans Home, New Orleans, Louisiana, Curt Teich & Co., Chicago, IL; Pg. 159 Belknaps Fountain, courtesy of The Historic New Orleans Collection; Pg. 159 Cistern, courtesy of The Historic New Orleans Collection; Pg. 159 Chess, Checkers & Whist Club, Library of Congress, Prints & Photographs Division, Detroit Publishing Company Collection; Pg. 160 Oldest Building, New Orleans, Frank B. Moore Collection, Earl K. Long Library, University of New Orleans; Pg. 161 Demolished cottage, Frank B. Moore Collection, Earl K. Long Library, University of New Orleans; Pg. 162 Girod Street Cemetery, photograph by Joe Bergeron, courtesy of Joe Bergeron; Pg. 163 Girod Street Cemetery, photograph by Joe Bergeron, courtesy of Joe Bergeron; Pg. 164-165 Rivergate, photograph by C. F. Weber, courtesy of Bergeron Gallery; Pg. 165 Errol Barron, Demolition of the Rivergate, 1994, courtesy of Errol Barron; Pg. 166 Aerial of Claiborne Avenue, courtesy of New Orleans Public Library; Pg. 167 Claiborne Oaks, courtesy of New Orleans Public Library; Pg. 168 Lee Circle Service Station, courtesy of The Historic New Orleans Collection; Pg. 169 St. Charles Avenue/Lee Circle showing Public Library and Lee's Monument (postcard), courtesy of The Historic New Orleans Collection; Pg. 169 St. Charles Avenue/Lee Circle showing Library and Shriners Temple (postcard), courtesy of The Historic New Orleans Collection; Pg. 170 Orleans Parish Criminal Courts Building, New Orleans, Louisiana, C. B. Mason, New Orleans

Completed in 1893, the Orleans Parish Criminal Court Building housed courts, police operations and a correctional facility. Though grand in stature, it was rife with structural problems. In the 1930s, the police headquarters and jail were relocated, the building becoming the locale for the Municipal Court, offices for the Works Progress Administration and a police precinct station. During that time, newspaper reporters discovered vagrants comfortably occupying the building's ground floor, thus nicknaming the structure the "Hotel de Bastille." The building was demolished in 1949. Today, the main branch of the New Orleans Public Library stands in its place at the corner of Tulane and Loyola Avenues.

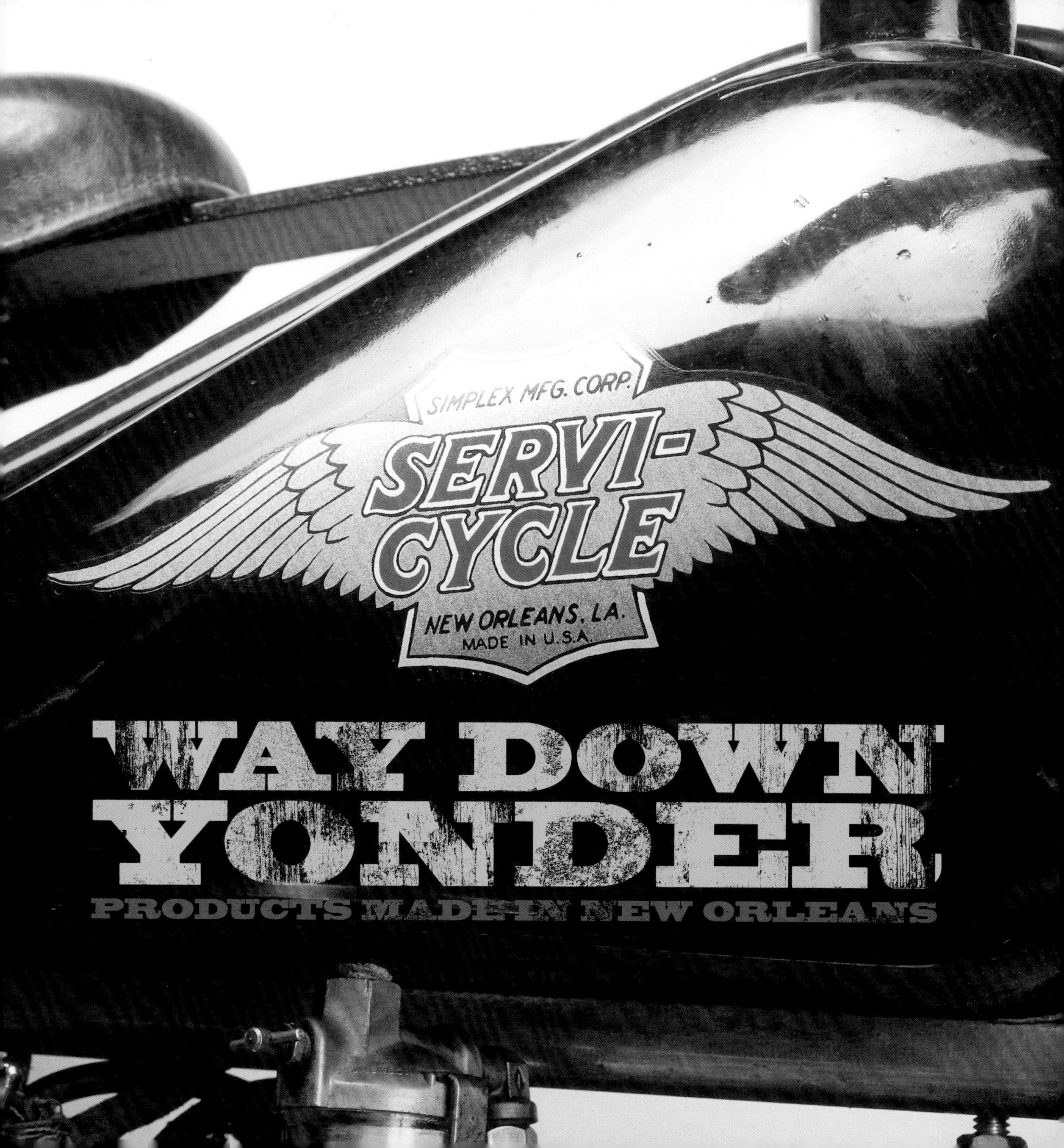

WAY DOWN YONDER

PRODUCTS MADE IN NEW ORLEANS

(Previous Page and Below) Located on Carrollton Avenue, the Simplex motorcycle company manufactured the Simplex Servi-Cycle, a small, lightweight motorcycle, from 1935 to 1960.

Since the steamboat era, when ships manufactured upriver altered the course of the city's history, New Orleans has been recognized as more of a commercial and shipping center than as a manufacturing center. Over the years, however, a diverse range of products and market brands have been associated with New Orleans and its evolving history. Memories and reminders of these products linger and are seen in a diverse range of signs, symbols, logos and labels. In some cases, these products suggested a sense of innovation and experimentation; in others, they reflected local traditions and a more refined local product.

Some of these, including the wide range of local beers and breweries, suggest the presence of distinctive and diverse nationalities in the city from an early era, as was evident with the Germans, who first arrived during the 18th century. Today landmark buildings, including those of the Jax Brewery, the Falstaff Brewery and the Dixie Brewing Company, stand as symbols of an era when more than 30 breweries and a diverse range of beer gardens, including Tivoli Gardens, thrived in New Orleans. Other city breweries included the Louisiana Brewery, the Eagle Brewery, the Pelican Brewing Company, the Southern Brewery, the Old Canal Steam Brewery, the Hope Brewery, the Crescent Brewing Company, the Lafayette Brewing Company, the American Brewing Company, the Algiers Home Brewing Company, the Columbia Brewing Company and the Union Brewing Company.

Because of its prominence as a port and as a primary portal to the Caribbean, New Orleans has played a central role in the evolution of the coffee trade in the United States. During the antebellum era, New Orleans served as home to hundreds of coffee houses, establishing the foundations for the many coffee houses evident in the city today. A wide range of coffee importers and coffee roasters thrived in the city. The American Coffee Company, for example, founded in 1890 on South St. Peters Street, produced a number of brands including French Market, St. Charles, Honeymoon, French Opera, Tulane, Pointer, Dixieland, Loyola and Monteleone.

The banana trade also reflects the importance of New Orleans as a port and the relationship of New Orleans to Latin America. Importing bananas through the port of New Orleans began after the Civil War, and was prominently advanced during the 20th century by Samuel Zemurray, known as "Sam the Banana Man." His Hubbard-Zemurray Company (later Cuyamel Fruit Company) was established in New Orleans in 1902; by 1929, Zemurray's Cuyamel Fruit Company was bought by the United Fruit Company; and by 1933, Zemurray was elected general manager of United Fruit. For much of the 20th century, New Orleans served as a primary port for the "Great White Fleet" of the United Fruit Company.

Soft drinks and other liquid refreshments developed as part of the city's history, reflecting the need to respond to its seemingly ever-present heat and humidity. Before national and large regional brands dominated the market, there was a distinctive range of local products, including Dr. Nut and Cola-Hiball.

The people of New Orleans seemed to have developed a particular taste for root beer, evident in such local favorites as Pa-Poose Root Beer, and in one better known label that originated here, Barq's Root Beer, which was acquired by a leading national brand, leaving behind a local legacy and loyal consumers.

Tobacco shops once thrived across the city, filled with a diverse and wide-ranging number of offerings. The production of cigars in New Orleans, though not as prominent an industry here as in a city like Tampa, also reflected the city's strong ties to Cuba and its established Cuban community. Brands like La Belle Creole were a symbol of this history.

Beginning in the 1930s, New Orleans served as the home for the Simplex motorcycle company, founded by J. Paul Treen, who had started as a Harley Davidson dealer in Baton Rouge. Treen built and refined a modern manufacturing plant in the city to produce his small, lightweight motorcycle, the Simplex Servi-Cycle, first distributed in 1935. Simplex Direct Drive Servi-Cycles were used widely by Western Union messengers. During World War II, the company produced over 10,000 special "G" models for use by the United States military. The company continued after the war, but declined during the late 1950s.

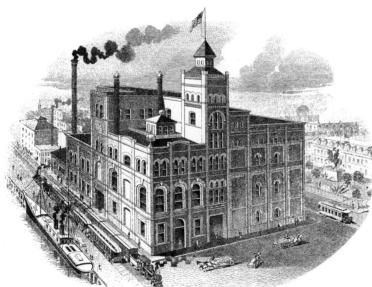

The Jax Brewery building was originally a rice mill, and was purchased in 1890 by an independent group of businessmen to establish the Jackson Brewery. The first beer — "Jax" — named for Andrew Jackson and the square located nearby that bears his name, was dispensed in 1891. Within a few years, restaurateur Lawrence Fabacher Sr. assumed control of the brewery, and the family continued to operate the business until its closing in 1974. Today the building, still called the Jax Brewery, is a retail complex.

With the slogan, "IT RUNS FOR MYLES," the Myles Salt Company, based in New Orleans, operated salt mines on both Avery Island and Weeks Island in Iberia Parish, Louisiana, west of New Orleans. The Avery Island mine passed out of Myles' hands in 1896, and the Weeks Island mine was sold to Morton Salt Company in 1947.

▸ In a bustling area located in the heart of downtown New Orleans, T. S. Waterman operated his business, manufacturing all things related to soda water, as depicted in this illustrated advertisement.

REGAL
BEER
BREWING COMPANY · NEW ORLEANS

Owned by the American Brewery Company, Regal Beer, called the "Prince of Golden Beers," was among the more popular beers brewed in New Orleans, beginning in 1890. Advertisments celebrated "red beans and rice and a Regal on ice," for the brew billed as "the never hurried beer." The brewery was also known for its women's professional softball team, the Regal Maids, reaching their own peak in popularity in the 1940's. Led by star player Claudia Yochim, sister of Major-leagers Lenny and Ray Yochim, the Maids were a tough ball club, second only to the Jax Girls, the national championship team, sponsored by local brewery competitor Jax Brewery. Regal Beer was a mainstay in the local brewery scene until 1962, where it operated in the building that is now the Royal Sonesta Hotel on Bourbon Street.

Among the several soft drinks produced by the World Bottling Company in the first half of the 20th century, Dr. Nut was unique for its name and almond taste. It gained notoriety for being the favorite drink of fictional character Ignatius Reilly from the Pulitzer-Prize winning novel *A Confederacy of Dunces* by New Orleans author John Kennedy Toole.

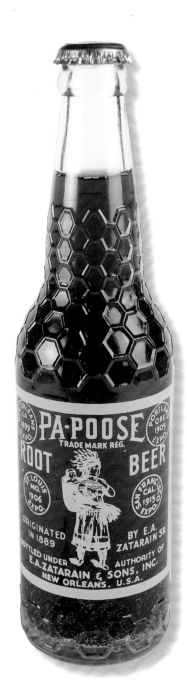

◀ The forerunner to the present-day Zatarain's, the company which has found its niche with New Orleans cooking, was Pa-Poose Products Company, started in 1889 by Emile A. Zatarain Sr.. His first product was root beer.

▶ The Cola Hiball was known as "the better drink."

MISSING NEW ORLEANS

▶ One constant in the city and through the port of New Orleans has been coffee. The local roasters and brands have varied through the years from the American Coffee Company's Tulane, Loyola and French Opera coffees to Valley Mills Company's Bourbon King.

NON PLUS ULTRA

La Belle Creole

▲ Mass production of cigars in New Orleans quickened with the building of the LaBelle Creole Cigar & Tobacco Factory in 1882, on the corner of Magazine and Julia streets. It was one of the largest factory buildings in New Orleans and at one time employed more than 1,200 workers. The building, which is a certified historic New Orleans landmark, still stands and is the home of the Deutsch, Kerrigan & Stiles law firm.

WAY DOWN YONDER: PRODUCTS MADE IN NEW ORLEANS

One of many soft drinks produced in New Orleans by the Cola-Hiball Company was the "Thirst Cola-Hiball," first introduced with the slogan "The better drink" in the early 1920s.

BUILDING ON THE PAST

SAZERAC COMPANY INC.

THE OGDEN MUSEUM OF SOUTHERN ART

THE HISTORIC NEW ORLEANS COLLECTION

SAZERAC COMPANY INC.

The Sazerac Company is one of the oldest family owned companies in New Orleans, dating back to the 1850s when the world famous "Sazerac" was prepared at the Sazerac Coffee House in the Vieux Carré, known as the French Quarter.

After leaving San Domingo, now Haiti, Antoine Amedie Peychaud arrived in New Orleans in 1795. Among the prized possessions he brought was a "secret" family recipe for making "bitters." That recipe would eventually become the world famous Peychaud's Bitters, still used today as the key ingredient in the perfect "Sazerac."

In 1838, Antoine Peychaud opened an apothecary at 123 Royal Street in the French Quarter. As part of his practice, he used his family's secret recipe for bitters as a natural cure for many ailments. Peychaud was a member of the Concorde Blue Lodge and his apothecary became a popular rendezvous for his fraternal brothers after lodge meetings. Peychaud would serve his evening guests brandy toddies, which included his secret blend of bitters. These toddies were served in a double-ended porcelain egg cup known as a *coquetier* (ko-k-tay). Due to the difficult pronunciation, the American's derived the words "cocktay" or "cocktail" to describe the drink — hence, America's first cocktail was born.

During the early 1800s, a number of saloons, veiled as "coffee houses," began lining the streets of the Vieux Carré. At that time, Sewell Taylor, a businessman, established the Merchants Exchange Coffee House, located at 16 Royal Street and 13 Exchange Place, on the corner of Exchange Alley. Taylor managed several coffee houses through the years.

In 1850, Taylor moved his businesses to 15-17 Royal Street, where he opened a liquor store. Thomas H. Handy, a young man from Maryland, was hired as a clerk. Handy did not stay with the business very long, instead enlisting with the Crescent City Heavy Artillery, but after three-and-a-half years of duty, returned to the liquor business.

▶ In the 1830s, Antoine Peychaud, who managed an apothecary in the French Quarter, used his family's secret recipe for Peychaud's Bitters not only as a natural cure for many ailments, but as a secret ingredient in brandy toddies he served to friends.

▶ Antoine Peychaud served brandy toddies to guests in a double-ended porcelain egg cup known as a *coquetier*.

▾ Peychaud's Bitters was bottled as a natural cure for many ailments and as an aromatic addition to a cocktail.

When Taylor moved his business and opened a liquor store on Royal Street, Aaron Bird moved into the old Merchant Exchange Coffee House. Bird renamed the business the Sazerac Coffee House, serving local Sazerac Coffee House patrons toddies made with a French brandy called *Sazerac-de-Forge et fils*. Bird also used Peychaud's Bitters in the toddy. The libation became known as the "Sazerac," and America had its first branded cocktail. Today, the Sazerac remains the official libation of the Krewe of Rex, the King of Carnival.

In 1857, Taylor confined his business to liquor retail and began advertising "Sazerac Brandy." Two years later, John B. Schiller became Bird's partner. Schiller became the sole owner of the Sazerac Coffee House and hired Handy as the clerk.

Upon Schiller's death in 1869, sale of the Coffee House was offered to Handy, per Schiller's will. As Handy took over as proprietor, Antoine Peychaud decided to close his apothecary and work for Handy. Peychaud was in charge of making his famous bitters at the Sazerac Coffee House, while Handy managed the business and marketing.

◄ Bar of The Old Absinthe House

In 1871, Handy opened a second business, the Thomas Handy Co., at 11 Exchange Place. As the proprietor of the Sazerac Coffee House, located at 14-16 Royal Street, Handy promoted the new business as the importer of Sazerac Brandy, wines and liquors. In 1873, he altered the recipe for the "Sazerac," replacing French brandy with American rye whiskey. A dash of absinthe was added to the "Sazerac." That same year, Handy acquired the formula for Peychaud Bitters from Antoine Peychaud.

In 1879, Handy lost the Sazerac Coffee House because of financial troubles. One of his employees, Vincent Micas, was able to gain control of the business. Later, William McQuoid helped Handy out of his financial difficulties, and in 1882 Handy regained control of the Sazerac Coffee House. He began to operate it and his associated businesses, under the ownership of McQuoid. Micas, after losing control of the Coffee House, began producing his own version of Peychaud's Bitters, and maintained a saloon, also known as the Sazerac House, at 116 Common Street. Micas' business changed hands several times and by 1886 was owned by Bauman and Jung Eventually, it was transferred to L. E. Jung and Wolff, a.k.a. Jung and Wolff.

Handy died in 1893, and his will requested McQuoid not change the name of the Sazerac business. McQuoid honored Handy's request and in 1896, the Sazerac business was enlarged to 12 & 13

◀ J. Marion Legendre and Reginald Parker first made absinthe in their basement, before labeling it "Herbsaint" and bottling it for distribution.

Royal Street. During that time, Peychaud's Bitters gained popularity, selling more than 800 cases per year. Sometime later, McQuiod chartered a new business, Thomas Handy & Co. Limited.

In 1919, the Sazerac Coffee House closed and the manufacturing of Peychaud's Bitters ceased because of Prohibition. William McQuoid passed ownership of the company to Christopher O'Reilly, and Thomas Handy & Co. was reorganized as the Sazerac Company. The new company survived Prohibition by billing itself as a "grocer and delicatessen." The business also expanded to include 116-118-120 Royal Street. At the end of Prohibition, the Sazerac Company moved from Royal Street to 722 Gravier Street and began producing Bitters again.

During World War I, two men, J. Marion Legendre and Reginald Parker, attended Intelligence school in Le Harve, France. After graduation, Parker traveled to Marseille and stayed with a family who had a special recipe for making pastis, or absinthe. Parker learned the art and, in 1918, returned with the recipe and ingredients to make the special absinthe. A year later, during Prohibition, Parker was reunited with Legendre. They began to make absinthe in their basement.

▲ At the turn of the 20th century, the Sazarac Bar moved from the French Quarter to the city's Central Business District, at the intersection of Gravier and Carondolet Streets, pictured here in the 1930s. Bartenders served patrons America's first cocktail, the Sazerac, for just 20¢ in those days. But Prohibition dealt the establishment a blow it never fully recovered from, and in 1949, the century-old tavern closed. When the Fairmont chain of luxury hotels acquired the Roosevelt in the 1950s, the bar was rescued, and today remains a popular destination for locals and tourists in the Fairmont New Orleans.

◀ The perfect Sazerac, celebrated in this book from the Sazerac Bar in the Roosevelt Hotel, includes a dash of Herbsaint. (Courtesy of the Fairmont Hotel, New Orleans)

After Prohibition was repealed, Legendre continued to make the absinthe he now called "herbsaint," pronounced erb-sant, in the attic of his home in New Orleans, located on Jefferson and Daneel. Herbsaint was taken from the New Orleans word for wormwood or *Herbe Sainte*. Wormwood was an ingredient used in Parker's recipe. In 1934, Legendre moved his Herbsaint production, first to 126 Baronne Street and then to 123 South Peters in 1935. Legendre hired Gus Blancand as a sales manager, and the spirit quickly became popular in San Fransisco, Chicago, Los Angeles and New Orleans. The Herbsaint recipe was handed down through the family and never altered through the years.

In 1948, the Goldring Family acquired the Sazerac Company from Christopher O'Reilly and moved it to 2237 Decatur Street. The business grew and the company moved again to 3735 Bienville Street.

In 1949, the Sazerac Company acquired the J. M. Legendre Co. and the rights to Herbaint, America's original absinthe. The official Sazerac cocktail recipe listed Herbsaint as the cocktail's absinthe. Herbsaint is now manufactured by the Sazerac Company. It is the only drink of its kind, and the perfect "Sazerac" now includes a dash of Herbsaint.

In 1970, the Sazerac Company acquired Peychaud's Bitters business, then owned by the Schenley Company, d.b.a. L. E. Jung and Wolff, Co. Sazerac became the "exclusive" maker and marketer of Peychaud's Bitters. Today it is known world-wide and used in many cocktail and food recipes.

In 1979, the Sazerac Company moved to its current location at 803 Jefferson Highway in New Orleans. Since that time, the Sazerac Company has acquired the Buffalo Trace Distillery, located in Frankfort, Kentucky, which supplied the rye whiskey to the Sazerac Coffee House in the late 1800s. Buffalo Trace Distillery specializes in producing and marketing high-end specialty bourbons such as Buffalo Trace, Van Winkle, Eagle Rare and George T. Stagg.

In 1999, the Sazerac Company acquired W. L. Weller and Old Charter Bourbons, completed the renovations of the Buffalo Trace Distillery and launched Buffalo Trace Bourbon. It also started making Sazerac Rye whiskey again so that aficionados around the world can enjoy a perfect "Sazerac," the world's finest cocktail and a true New Orleans original.

All images courtesy of Sazerac Company, Inc. unless otherwise noted.

THE OGDEN MUSEUM OF SOUTHERN ART

▲ H.H. Richardson's Neo-Romanesque style, as seen in the Patrick F. Taylor Library, is characterized by massive stone walls and turrets, as depicted on this postcard.

▼ Noel Rockmore's portrait of *Bill Matthews* is one of a series of nearly 200 paintings the artist rendered in the early 1960s of old jazz musicians who played at Preservation Hall.
(Ogden Museum Permanent Collection)

In 1994, an ambitious vision was announced – the creation of a museum that would serve as the premier national resource on the visual arts and culture of the American South – The Ogden Museum of Southern Art, University of New Orleans.

Additionally, it was hoped that the Museum, located on historic Lee Circle, would launch the revitalization of Lee Circle and its development into a major cultural center for the South, as well as a portal to the city's historic Warehouse District.

Today, the first phase of that vision has been realized with the opening of Stephen Goldring Hall (2003), one of three buildings comprising the Museum complex, where the 20th and 21st century collections are showcased. This contemporary glass, concrete and stone structure was designed by the New Orleans architectural firm of Barron & Toups to complement the historic neighborhood in which the museum is located.

The Ogden Museum's landmark structure, and its cornerstone building, is the historic 1889 library building designed by New Orleans native Henry Hobson Richardson, one of America's greatest architects. Today, the building, known as the Patrick F. Taylor Library, is the focus of an extensive preservation and adaptive reuse project. It is recognized as one of New Orleans' major urban development projects.

The Library was constructed on Lee Circle during a period of time when the city was enjoying a late 19th century renaissance. City officials had recently hosted the 1884-85 World's Industrial and Cotton Centennial Exposition in Audubon Park. New buildings were being constructed uptown and in other parts of the city, and the lakefront, with its popular venues West End Park and Spanish Fort, was enjoying an increase in visitation with the advent of transportation to the city's northern end. The St. Charles Avenue streetcar line was established; steamboats were lining the Mississippi River levee, and train travel to and from the city was on the rise.

Originally built as the Howard Memorial Library, this landmark building was the last of six libraries designed by Henry Hobson Richardson, one of the trinity of modern American architects, along with Louis Sullivan and Frank Lloyd Wright. It was built by the Howard family, an influential New Orleans family.

Listed on the National Historic Register, this 1889 building is an example of Richardson's Neo-Romanesque style, characterized by massive stone walls, turrets, semi-circular arches and detailed interior millwork. The building served as a library for over 50 years, but ceased service as a library completely in 1939. During the ensuing years, it was converted to a radio station, and later to corporate offices.

Following a fire in 1945, the structure underwent a series of drastic modifications that destroyed much of the building's original interior. The painstaking restoration work in the 1980s by Barron & Toups brought back the Library's majestic reading room, easily one of the most impressive late 19th century interior spaces in Louisiana.

▲ The rotunda of the H.H. Richardson designed Patrick F. Taylor Library is rich with detailed interior millwork.

Stephen Goldring Hall (photograph by Jack Kotz)

Barron & Toups continues to direct the Library's restoration, and when complete this architectural treasure will stand, once again, as Richardson intended - as a work of art in itself.

The Library will house works by artists including William Henry Buck, Richard Clague, Alexander Drysdale, Joseph Rusling Meeker, Julian Onderdonk, Thomas Sully, George David Coulon, Lulu King Saxon, George Ohr, William Woodward and Ellsworth Woodward. The galleries will feature landscapes, portraits and nautical themes, as well as art depicting old New Orleans, old Texas and the Civil War. The Taylor Library will also house the multi-media orientation theater, a computer resource center and the permanent home of the Goldring-Woldenberg Institute for the Advancement of Southern Art and Culture.

Adjoining the library will be the newly-constructed Clementine Hunter Education Wing, named to honor the spirit and creativity of this renowned Louisiana self-taught artist. The granddaughter of a former slave, she began painting life as she knew it in her mid-50s. She lived most of her life on Melrose Plantation in Natchitoches, Louisiana. The Education Wing will house 19th and early 20th century galleries and a teacher/docent resource center, as well as the Wisner Foundation Education Center with classrooms and studio spaces, critical to the Museum's educational mission.

Since its opening, the Museum has showcased art representing 15 Southern states and the District of Columbia, featuring works from 1890 to the present day. The newly opened Ogden Museum has developed as a center for education and a place to celebrate the unique culture of the South, its history, literature, music, food and spirit … and increasingly, it is regarded as "More than a Museum."

THE HISTORIC NEW ORLEANS COLLECTION

The Historic New Orleans Collection is honored to join its sister institution, The Ogden Museum of Southern Art, in supporting the reissue of *Missing New Orleans*. Our staff and board of directors, like so many readers, have been touched by this work, and we welcome the opportunity to introduce an even larger audience to this timely, timeless book.

Located in a historic complex of French Quarter buildings, The Historic New Orleans Collection was established in 1966 by General and Mrs. L. Kemper Williams to maintain and expand their collection of Louisiana materials and make it available to the public. Headquartered at 533 Royal Street, the museum opened in May, 1970. The complex is anchored by the Merieult House, built in 1792 by merchant-trader Jean Francois Merieult. A regional landmark, the Merieult House survived the great fire of 1794 and is one of the very few Vieux Carré structures remaining from the Spanish colonial period. In 1938, at the urging of French Quarter preservationists, the Williamses purchased the Merieult House and a late-19th-century residence facing Toulouse Street. Five additional buildings contiguous to the Merieult plot, and linked by interior courtyards, now accommodate staff offices and exhibition space. Nearby, at 410 Chartres Street, stands the Williams Research Center — a Beaux Arts structure erected in 1915 to serve as the Second City Criminal Court and the Third District Police Station. Restored and opened to the public in 1996, the Williams Research Center houses The Collection's reading room as well as offices for curatorial, library, and manuscripts personnel and collection storage and processing areas.

Visitors to The Collection venture upon a thoroughfare spanning five centuries of exploration, settlement, and cultural innovation. Prized collections include the William C. Cook War of 1812 in the South Collection; the Bill Russell Jazz Collection; the Fred W. Todd Tennessee Williams Collection; and the photographic archives of J. D. Edwards, Eugene Delcroix, and Clarence John Laughlin. The Historic New Orleans Collection's matchless visual holdings compel visitors to gaze, ponder and discover, in Laughlin's words, "evidences of an amazing, and indigenous, kind of fantasy which sprang into being here, evidences which are to be found still, if they are carefully searched for, in the 'lost' streets, the strange burial grounds, the impossibly decayed houses of old New Orleans." We stroll down these streets, as we page through this book, in search of internal and external verities. Nearly one in three historical images featured in *Missing New Orleans* has been drawn from Collection holdings. Each has the capacity to change our perception of self and city.

▲ *Detail of Merieult House Courtyard,*
The Historic New Orleans Collection
2005
photograph by Jan White Brantley
Many French Quarter buildings feature interior courtyards. The Merieult House courtyard is one of three lush courtyards in the Royal Street complex.

▲ *Reading Room, Williams Research Center*
410 Chartres Street
1996
photograph by Jan White Brantley

Change, of course, is one of the themes of *Missing New Orleans*. And change, as we know, often registers as loss. It needn't. This book entreats all of us — New Orleans natives, adoptive sons and daughters, far-flung devotees — to transmute loss into possession. Not a simple process, but a vital one, and a central mission of cultural institutions such as The Historic New Orleans Collection.

Santayana had it wrong when he claimed that those who cannot remember the past are condemned to repeat it. Or perhaps he had the story right, but the moral wrong. There are times, particularly times of upheaval, when we *yearn* to repeat the past. We seek continuity, we revere tradition. But unless our traditions remain accessible, vital, and permutable, they are already good as lost.

What does it mean to miss New Orleans? In *Missing New Orleans'* formulation, it has a little to do with memory and a lot to do with maturation. Therein lies the message of hope in this text, and in the post-Katrina landscape. Loss is inevitable. But as we grow up, and grow wise, we learn how to remember.

We must all learn to strike a balance between past and future, nostalgia and curiosity. We urge you to visit The Historic New Orleans Collection. And then we urge you to go back out into the streets of New Orleans and create new memories, new images, new poems, new songs. In that way, New Orleans will forever be renewed.

▲ *The Jelly Roll Blues*
1915; sheet music cover
Ferdinand Morton, composer; sheet music for piano by Will Rossiter
William Russell Jazz Collection
Clarisse Claiborne Grima Fund Purchase

▲ *Canal Street, East of Royal Street, North Side*
between 1857 and 1860; salted paper
photoprint by Jay Dearborn Edwards
1982.32.3
This photograph of the current 400–600 blocks of Canal Street (from Royal to North Peters) was made in the years just prior to the Civil War by Jay Dearborn Edwards, whose images are the earliest known paper photographs of New Orleans. In the distance, the United States Customs House, covered with scaffolding, is under construction.

▲ *Clara de la Motte*
ca. 1795; oil on canvas by José Francisco de Salazar y Mendoza
1981.213
In 1787, Clara de la Motte arrived in New Orleans from Curaçao to wed Benjamin Monsanto. The couple was among the earliest Jewish residents of New Orleans. The artist José Francisco de Salazar y Mendoza, active in the Crescent City from 1782 until his death in 1802, is the earliest known portraitist in New Orleans.

PHILLIP COLLIER

Phillip Collier was born in Wetumpka, Alabama and grew up in nearby Montgomery. He earned a B.F.A. in visual design from Auburn University. After working in Birmingham for a short time, he moved to New Orleans to work as a freelance illustrator, art and creative director, before establishing his own firm, Phillip Collier Designs, in 1990. Local clients include Arthur Roger Gallery, Louisiana Philharmonic Orchestra, Louisiana ArtWorks and Mignon Faget. National clients have included the Palmer House Hotel (Chicago), the Waldorf Astoria (New York), CBS Sports Radio, Sprint and TABASCO®. Collier has won many local, regional and national design awards and was selected to create the official poster of the 1980 New Orleans Jazz and Heritage Festival, which was chosen for the cover of the *Library of Congress Quarterly* magazine and was included in the Library of Congress' 100-year Retrospective on the History of Posters, at home in the Washington, D.C. permanent collection. He is currently designing a book on the history of TABASCO®, with design associate Scott Carroll, slated for publication in 2006.

J. RICHARD GRUBER

J. Richard Gruber, Ph.D. was appointed Director of The Ogden Museum of Southern Art in 1999. Prior to joining the Ogden Museum, he served as Deputy Director for the Morris Museum of Art and as the founding Director of its Center for the Study of Southern Painting in Augusta, Georgia. He has also been Director of the Memphis Brooks Museum of Art in Memphis, Tennessee, Director of the Wichita Art Museum in Wichita, Kansas, and Director of the Peter Joseph Gallery in New York. After graduating from Xavier University in Cincinnati, Ohio, he earned an M.A. degree in art history from the University of Colorado at Boulder, then a M.Ph. and Ph.D. in art history from the University of Kansas at Lawrence. He was awarded a Kress Foundation Fellowship and a Smithsonian Pre-Doctoral Research Fellowship at the National Museum of Art. Active as a curator and author, he has published books and catalogs, including *Thomas Hart Benton and the American South; American Icons; From Madison to Manhattan: The Art of Benny Andrews.*

JIM RAPIER

A native and resident of New Orleans, Jim Rapier earned a B.A. in English from Hampden-Sydney College in Virginia. He served as a reporter for the *Daily Advance* in Elizabeth City, North Carolina. Jim and his wife, Marion, live in New Orleans, where he has been a reporter for the *Times-Picayune* since 1995.

MARY BETH ROMIG

Mary Beth Romig is the Public Information Officer for The Ogden Museum of Southern Art. She earned a B.A. in English and Secondary Education from the University of New Orleans. Romig served as Managing Editor of *New Orleans Magazine, Louisiana Life,* and *Our Kids Magazine,* where she was a contributing writer. She has also worked for Special Olympics International, Tulane University, and as the Public Relations Director for St. Mary's Dominican High School. Romig is a native New Orleanian, and lives in the city with her husband, Cecil Haskins, and daughter, Lindsey.

BRENNAN'S PRINTING

Brennan's House of Printing, Inc., founded by Robert M. Brennan, started its presses in 1972. In 1980, he turned over the management of the company to his son, Danny, and under his direction and with his passion for printing the company grew to new heights. Now, in its 3rd generation, Brennan's has retained Danny's vision of being an innovative printing company providing outstanding customer service and a quality product. Family-owned and operated in metropolitan New Orleans, Brennan's has continued to invest in the latest printing technology and equipment and has a reputation for meeting the ever-changing needs of its clients. Brennan's continues to grow by offering its customers full pre-press services, digital four-color printing, full-color conventional offset printing, bindery and complete mailing services. The name, as well as the spirit of Danny Brennan, lives on in Brennan's Printing today.

INDEX

HOTEL DIEU, NEW ORLEANS, LA.

In 1859, the Daughters of Charity founded, owned and operated Hotel Dieu hospital, its original name meaning "House of God." It began with the care of five patients and was the only private hospital in New Orleans in operation during the Civil War. The original structure, located on Tulane Avenue near Gravier Street, was replaced in 1924, and in 1972 that building was torn down to make way for a more modern structure. In late 1992, the Daughters of Charity sold the hospital to the state of Louisiana, at the request of the Governor Edwin Edwards' administration. It was renamed University Hospital, and became a sister institution to Charity Hospital, founded in 1736 and one of the oldest public hospitals in the nation.

FURTHER READING

Asbury, Herbert. *The French Quarter: An Informal History of the New Orleans Underworld*. New York, NY: Thunder's Mouth Press, 1936.

Branley, Edward J. *New Orleans: The Canal Streetcar Line*. Images of America. Charleston, SC: Arcadia Publishing, 1999.

Brock, Eric J. *New Orleans*. Images of America. Charleston, SC: Arcadia Publishing, 2004.

Brock, Eric J. *New Orleans Cemeteries*. Images of America. Charleston, SC: Arcadia Publishing, 2004.

Cable, Mary. *Lost New Orleans*. Boston, MA: Houghton Mifflin Co., 1980.

Campanella, Richard. *Time and Place in New Orleans: Past Geographies in the Present Day*. Gretna, LA: Pelican Publishing Company, Inc., 2002.

Campanella, Richard and Marina. *New Orleans: Then and Now*. Gretna, LA: Pelican Publishing Company, Inc., 1999.

Chase, John Churchill. *Frenchmen, Desire, Good Children: And Other Streets of New Orleans*. Third Edition. New York, NY: Simon and Schuster, 1949.

Clifford, Jan and Leslie Blackshear Smith. *The Incomplete, Year-By-Year, Selectively Quirky, Prime Facts Edition of the History of the New Orleans Jazz and Heritage Festival*. New Orleans, LA: e/Prime Publications, 2005.

Faragher, Scott. *New Orleans in Vintage Postcards*. (The Postcard History Series). Charleston, SC: Arcadia Publishing, 1999.

Federal Writers' Project of the Works Progress Administration for the City of New Orleans. *New Orleans City Guide*. American Guide Series. Boston, MA: Houghton Mifflin Company, 1938.

Fox, F. G. *Bizarre: New Orleans*. New Orleans, LA: St. Expedite Press, 1997.

Hearn, Lafcadio. *Sketches of New Orleans*. Franklin, NH: Hillside Press, 1964.

Huber, Leonard V. *New Orleans: A Pictorial History*. New York, NY: Crown Publishers, Inc., 1971.

Kelman, Ari; *A River and Its City: The Nature of Landscape in New Orleans*. Berkley, Los Angeles, CA: University of California Press, 2003.

Kemp, John R. *New Orleans*. Woodland Hills, CA: Windsor Publications, Inc. 1981.

Lachoff, Irwin and Catherine C. Kahn. *The Jewish Community of New Orleans*. Images of America. Charleston, SC: Arcadia Publishing, 2005.

Leavitt, Mel. *A Short History of New Orleans*. San Francisco, CA: LEXIKOS, 1982.

Lewis, Peirce F. *New Orleans: The Making of an Urban Landscape*. Santa Fe, NM and Harrisonburg, VA: The University of Virginia Press, 2003.

Long, Alecia P. *The Great Southern Babylon: Sex, Race, and Respectability in New Orleans, 1865-1920*. Baton Rouge, LA: Louisiana University Press, 2004.

Long, Judy, editor. *Literary New Orleans*. Athens, GA: Hill Street Press, 1999.

Maselli, Joseph and Dominic Candeloro. *Italians in New Orleans*. Images of America. Charleston, SC: Arcadia Publishing, 2004.

Merrill, Ellen C. *Germans of Louisiana*. Gretna, LA: Pelican Publishing Company, 2005.

Reeves, Sally K. Evans and William D. Reeves. *History of City Park, New Orleans*. New Orleans, LA: City Park Improvement Association and the Friends of City Park, 2000.

Rose, Al. *Storyville, New Orleans. Being An Authentic, Illustrated Account of the Notorious Red-Light District*. Tuscaloosa, AL and London, England: The University of Alabama Press, 1974.

Rose, Al and Edmond Souchon, *New Orleans Jazz: A Family Album*. Baton Rouge, LA: Louisiana State University Press, 1967.

Starr, S. Frederick. *Southern Comfort: The Garden District of New Orleans*. New York, NY: Princeton Architectural Press, 1998.

Saxon, Lyle, Edward Dreyer and Robert Tallant. *Gumbo Ya-Ya: A Collection of Louisiana Folk Tales*. Gretna, LA: Pelican Publishing Company, 1987.

Sullivan, Lester. *New Orleans Then and Now*. San Diego, CA: Thunder Bay Press, 2003.

Twain, Mark. *Life on the Mississippi* (Vol. 9). New York, NY and London, England: Harper Brothers Publishers, 1874.

Widmer, Mary Lou. *New Orleans in the Thirties*. Gretna, LA: Pelican Publishing Company, Inc., 1989.

Widmer, Mary Lou. *New Orleans in the Forties*. Gretna, LA: Pelican Publishing Company, Inc., 1990.

Widmer, Mary Lou. *New Orleans in the Fifties*. Gretna, LA: Pelican Publishing Company, Inc., 1991.

Widmer, Mary Lou. *New Orleans in the Twenties*. Gretna, LA: Pelican Publishing Company, Inc., 1993.

Wilson, Samuel Jr., Patricia Brady and Lynn D. Adams, editors. *Queen of the South: New Orleans, 1853-1862, The Journal of Thomas K. Wharton*. New Orleans, LA: The Historic New Orleans Collection, 1999.

Author unknown. *A Guide to the Historic Shops and Restaurants of New Orleans*. Distributed by Publishers Group West. New York, NY: The Little Bookroom, 2004.

In 1878, Thomas Sydenham Hardee delineated the map, entitled *Topographical and Drainage Map of New Orleans and Surroundings from Recent Surveys and Investigations*, showing where most of the city's then 200,000 residents had settled along the natural levees of the Mississippi River, created by sediment built up from periodic flooding. Almost every area of reclaimed marshland uninhabited in 1878 flooded in 2005, after the breaching and failure of the levee system across New Orleans. Lost to the floodwaters were many of the city's neighborhoods, including the historic lower Ninth Ward, the vast expanse of New Orleans East, Lakeview, City Park, Gentilly, Pigeontown, Gerttown, Central City, Mid-City and Broadmoor. (The 1878 Hardee Map of New Orleans used with permission from The Historic New Orleans Collection.)

Floodwaters near the I-610, Gentilly

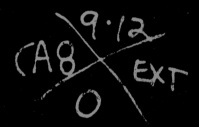

EPILOGUE

HURRICANE KATRINA
8/29/2005

Missing *New Orleans*, in its final proof form, was scheduled to be delivered to Brennan's Printing in New Orleans on Wednesday, August 31, 2005. Hurricane Katrina struck New Orleans and the Gulf Coast on Monday, August 29. Twenty-four hours after Katrina made landfall the New Orleans levee and canal system failed, including the 17th Street Canal, the London Avenue Canal and the Industrial Canal. Our definition of "missing" changed quickly and dramatically. The creators of this book, evacuees from New Orleans, relocated to Baton Rouge, Memphis, Houston, Palm Beach and Twin Lakes, Wisconsin. We watched as televised images immediately redefined what our title, *Missing New Orleans*, would literally come to mean for us and for hundreds of thousands of people scattered throughout the country.

In little more than 24 hours the entire landscape of a great American city was radically changed on an environmental and human scale. The litany of what remains missing is profound – people, families, friends, pets, homes, schools, entire neighborhoods and communities, city services, healthcare, buildings, businesses and industry, long-held traditions and the simplest routines of daily life.

We evacuated, our heads filled with details - facts, names and dates about this great city. Our focus on the original book had been on individual buildings, businesses, traditions and pleasures; our definition would now have to be broadened to include missing elements that are too profound to comprehend, too difficult to put into perspective.

A poignant question was posed on the local *Times-Picayune's* Web site: "What happened to my neighborhood?" In some cases - the Lower Ninth Ward, Lakeview, New Orleans East, Gentilly, parts of Plaquemines Parish, the entirety of St. Bernard, and much of Mississippi Gulf Coast - the answer was sweeping devastation. Flood waters and wind spared few homes and businesses in these areas. Every neighborhood in the metropolitan area, on the city's Northshore, and east along the Mississippi Gulf Coast was affected.

Three of the principals involved in the creation of this book returned to the city to discover the loss of their homes in the hard-hit Lakeview neighborhood. In the midst of that personal loss, as we worked to keep the Ogden Museum and our businesses afloat in an extremely challenging environment, we grappled with questions as to how to proceed with completing the book project. As this national tragedy continued to unfold, amid the varying levels of human loss, should we proceed with publishing at all? And if so, should we address the issue of this new definition of "missing" and the devastation from Katrina?

Phillip Collier, the originator of *Missing New Orleans*, has worked on this book for years. He is among those who fell in love with this city and moved here. Some of us are natives who simply don't want to live anywhere else. All of us have experienced something few have faced in the past – a natural disaster of this magnitude, perhaps the greatest in the history of the United States. We explored many options, via phone and e-mail, before we were able to return to New Orleans. During this period we learned that our colleague, David Rae Morris, a photographer whose work is included in the Ogden Museum's Permanent Collection, was working in the affected areas, capturing images in the metropolitan New Orleans and

Louisiana Superdome, Central Business District

Toxic art on the neutral ground, Bywater

the Mississippi Gulf Coast. Morris' family ties trace back to Mississippi, and his most recent book, *My Mississippi*, published with his father, Willie Morris, documented the same coastal areas affected by the storm.

As image after image appeared, we realized that these remarkable photographs, created by an individual whose home and studio is located in New Orleans, while documenting the harsh facts, were also proving to be a personal record of the many levels of damage and destruction taking place throughout the entire area affected by Katrina.

Before Katrina, this book project taught us that New Orleans survives, no matter the challenges from man or nature. It is a tenacious city that has survived plagues, fires, foreign attacks and other natural disasters. It is a place that basks in humidity and its own brand of elegance, decadence and decay, a city rich in tradition, seductive, sultry and sweet. It is a city

National Guard convoy on St. Charles Avenue, Uptown

that is also steeped in family tradition, and people with ties to single neighborhoods dating back generations. It boasts its own *laissez faire* lifestyle and a deeply rooted funkiness.

Nothing has challenged the city on this scale since it was founded in 1718. The facts and figures about the loss and devastation have been reported and will enter the public record. But it is the personal stories that will tell the most.

Damaged steeple of Trinity Lutheran Church, Algiers

This epilogue is dedicated to all those who had to leave because of Hurricane Katrina, and who now know what it means to truly miss New Orleans, to those who remained so that people can and will again return, and to those who came from across the country to assist our various local law enforcement and social service agencies to ensure that New Orleans' history and cultural heritage will be preserved for future generations.

As *Missing New Orleans* goes to print, the story continues to unfold, with the script for the future continuing to be written. What will remain missing is yet to be determined.

Flooding of the St. Bernard Housing Project, Gentilly

EPILOGUE

Flooding of St. Louis Cemetery, Tremé

National Guard on patrol on Decatur Street, French Quarter

Debris field by the U.S. Coast Guard Station in Bucktown near the 17th Street Canal breach, Metairie

Storm debris and devastation in Lower Ninth Ward
and a stray dog in Upper Ninth Ward

Boarded up-window on Magazine Street, Uptown

Burned-out warehouse near the Mississippi River with New Orleans skyline, Bywater

Burned-out warehouse along Chartres Street, Bywater

Barge near breach in the Industrial Canal, Lower Ninth Ward

EPILOGUE

Search and rescue markings, Lower Ninth Ward

Fats' Domino's home, Lower Ninth Ward

Search and rescue along Humanity Street, Gentilly

EPILOGUE

Search and rescue near the breach of the 17th Street canal, Lakeview

Remains of the West End Lighthouse, New Orleans Lakefront

Antique car in drying muck, Lower Ninth Ward

Biloxi Lighthouse with pile of debris, Biloxi, Mississippi

Beach Boulevard, Bay St. Louis, Mississippi

American flag among debris along beachfront, Bay St. Louis, Mississippi

EPILOGUE

Remaining slab, Waveland, Mississippi

First Baptist Church, Bay St. Louis, Mississippi

Railroad bridge, Bay St. Louis, Mississippi

Patrick Hotard, Curator, at the remains of the front gate of
Jefferson Davis' home, Beauvoir, Biloxi, Mississippi

Morris' home, Bywater

David Rae Morris was born in Oxford, England and grew up in New York City. He had an early interest in photography and attended night classes at the International Center of Photography. He holds a B.A. from Hampshire College in Amherst, Massachusetts, and an M.A. in Journalism and Mass Communication from the University of Minnesota. His photographs have been published in such diverse publications as *Time Magazine*, *Newsweek*, *USA Today*, and the *New York Times*, the *Angolite*, the official Magazine of the Louisiana State Penitentiary at Angola, and *Love and Rage*, a national anarchist weekly. He had also served as a contributing photographer for the Associated Press, Reuters, and Agency France Presse.

In 1999, Morris collaborated with his late father, the noted author Willie Morris, on *My Mississippi*, a collection of essays and photographs about the state of Mississippi and her people, published by the University Press of Mississippi. His photographs are in many private and public collections including in the permanent collections of the Ogden Museum of Southern Art in New Orleans and Mississippi Museum of Art in Jackson.

Morris and his long time partner, Susanne Dietzel, have lived in New Orleans since 1994. They have a four-year-old daughter, Uma Rae Morris Dietzel.